DAY BY DAY

D1614289

DAY BY DAY

WITH MY DAILY VISITOR

**compiled and
edited by
Patrick R. Moran**

Our Sunday Visitor, Inc.
Huntington, Indiana 46750

The daily scriptural verses were reprinted from the Holy Bible, Revised Standard Version, Catholic Edition, © 1966 by Division of Christian Education of the National Council of Churches of Christ in the United States of America.
Thomas Nelson & Sons, publisher.

Copyright © 1980 by Our Sunday Visitor, Inc.

All rights reserved. No part of this book may be reproduced or copied in any form or by any means — graphic, electronic, or mechanical, including photocopying, recording, taping, or information storage and retrieval systems — without written permission of the publisher.

ISBN: 0-87973-530-9

Library of Congress Catalog Card Number: 79-92536

Cover Photos by John A. Zierten
Cover Design by James E. McIlrath

Published, printed and bound in the United States of America

Editor's Preface

MY DAILY VISITOR, a pocket-sized booklet of prayers and reflections, has provided daily spiritual reading for thousands of subscribers since its inception in February 1957.

Now in full-sized book format, DAY BY DAY WITH MY DAILY VISITOR is designed to be a welcome visitor in the home, providing its readers with spiritual writings, meditations and reflections for each day of the year. The selections are compiled from past issues of MY DAILY VISITOR, bringing to its readers a 22-year selection of the best in spiritual thoughts. Perhaps your favorite is among these.

The index of writers reads like a "Who's Who" among Catholic hierarchy, cleric and lay editors, authors, preachers, and radio and television personalities. You will be certain to recognize many popular "visitors" from bygone as well as contemporary times.

The 366 daily entries are presented in a monthly chronological fashion, with many of the reflections centering on principal feast days of the Saints, and on the liturgical seasons of the Church. Other reflections focus upon specific events, personalities, and holidays of a patriotic or seasonal appeal. This almanac of inspirational thoughts will guide the reader through the joys and blessings of the birth of spring, the growth of summer, the beauty of autumn, and the dormancy of a snow-blanketed winter.

Certain readers among the subscribers of MY DAILY VISITOR, have voiced their favorite selections and themes. Of course, they also had preferences regarding the writers or guest editors. Readers will note a vast resource of reflections and thoughts of Our Blessed Mother contained among the daily entries. This is as it should be, since Marian reflections are one of the most popular themes in spiritual writing and thinking.

God's beauty is one of all seasons. His blessings are those of every day. DAY BY DAY WITH MY DAILY VISITOR shares these blessings with you, affording all the beauty of spiritual and inspirational thought. Let this book be your almanac and spiritual diary for each day of the year, and for years to follow.

—*Patrick R. Moran*

Foreword

The holiness to which each one of us is called consists not so much in external actions as in interior union with Jesus Christ. When Jesus approved the contemplation of Mary over Martha's hustle and bustle, He was telling each of us that we must take time out of busy days simply to be in His presence. He invites us to think about Him and to reflect on how His truth can live in our own lives. In short, what Jesus is inviting us to do is to meditate.

While most people would agree that it is good to meditate, and while most spiritual writers seem to indicate that some form of meditation is necessary for perfection, many of us have difficulty in getting started. We approach meditation with our minds as a blank slate, and we are not sure just what to put on it. We know that meditation is mental prayer that uses the memory, intellect, and will to arrive at a conclusion and resolution. Our main problem is how to begin, particularly what to meditate about.

This book can serve that purpose. Patrick Moran has gone through years of readings that have appeared in MY DAILY VISITOR, composed by some of the best spiritual writers in this country, and brought the best of them together in a book that has a meditation thought-starter for each day of the year.

These writings are not meditations in themselves, but they will provide us each day with a thought for consideration. It will be up to each one of us how best this thought can be applied to our own individual lives. The resolutions we make will be determined by our own needs, our state of life, and the inspirations of God's grace. There is a wonderful spiritual diversity in this book, and how we use it depends solely on our own ingenuity. Good meditating, and may you profit from it.

—*Albert J. Nevins, M.M.*

For the convenience of the reader,
an alphabetical listing
of contributors to
DAY BY DAY WITH MY DAILY VISITOR
can be found at the back of the book.

January 1

This month shall be for you the beginning of months; it shall be the first month of the year for you. —Exodus 12:2

A New Year begins today. Like the past year it will come to you one day at a time. Each of these days will present you with an opportunity to fulfill the reason for which you were placed on this earth. Be reminded that the prime reason for your existence here is simply the glorification of Almighty God.

HOW, WHEN AND WHERE you do this is something that you alone must decide. It is however, absolutely essential that you do glorify God according to your ability.

GOD DOES NOT expect the impossible. He does not even really care particularly for any great results. It is the motivation generating the act that interests Him. It is the intention behind the product that fascinates Him. In everything and anything that is done by His creatures, there is one thing and one thing only that He most ardently looks for and that is love.

—BISHOP ANDREW GRUTKA, Gary Indiana

January 2

For God alone my soul waits in silence; from him comes my salvation. —Psalms 62:1

TIME is given to us for one purpose — to work out our salvation. To use time, then, for sin is one of the greatest abuses of time. It was never intended for that end. Anybody who is in the state of sin is wasting time no matter what else he may be doing.

WHEN a person is in sin, it makes no difference how charitable he may appear; how meticulous he is in performing his daily task — all this is wasted time as far as eternity is concerned.

GOD intended for us to be in the state of grace at all times. Just as soon as we fall into sin and out of grace, we are in a condition never intended by God. From that point on we are abusing God's time and wasting our lives.

THE IMPRINT we make on time is the imprint that appears again in eternity. We will have to give an account of the time that God has given to us.

—FATHER ALBERT J. NIMETH, O.F.M.

January 3

Remember, O Lord, what the measure of life is, for what vanity thou hast created all the sons of men!   —Psalms 89:46

I AM scared. Yesterday I resolved to try again to do everything for love of God, and yet I goofed. I was cross. I complained. I did many things in anger or out of habit and almost nothing out of love. I forgot You. I am afraid to start again and fail again. I can't ever be a good Christian.

FOOLISH CHILD of God! Who can be good with ease? The great saints also tried and failed and feared and tried again and again. Your fear is part of the growth of your spirit; for fear of the Lord is the beginning of wisdom. Let your failures and fears help you to come nearer to God.

WHATEVER you do, give it to the Lord. Both failures and success He will receive with His steadfast love. In His wisdom He will use whatever you offer. Give Him what you have and are. If you do not have patience, give Him your impatience. If you do not have understanding, give Him your confusion. If you are not full of love, give Him your emptiness. He will use it all for good.

—BETTY WICKHAM

January 4

Humble yourselves before the Lord and he will exalt you.

—James 4:10

I T is good to know that there are American saints, and perhaps we shall see more of them as our second centenary approaches. Most of the saints we know are European far removed from our time and place.

NOT SO Saint Elizabeth Seton. She lived in Baltimore. She was a wife and mother, and a teaching nun. These things are familiar and close to us. She lived and worked not too long ago and she was the kind of person who might be teaching in our school.

SAINTS are not really much different from ourselves, and often in their lifetimes did not appear very different to some people. But, deep down, they were extraordinarily different, and that is why they were saints. They took their God and their faith very seriously. Saint Elizabeth Ann Seton spoke our language and walked on our native soil. This proclaims that holiness is not far from every one of us, and is in the reach of all.

—FATHER BLASE SCHAUER, O.P.

January 5

It is better to be of lowly spirit with the poor than to divide the spoil with the proud. —Proverbs 16:19

NAPOLEON'S uniform coat, captured at the battle of Waterloo, was sold for $38,000. It was placed in the Wellington Museum at Stratfield Saye House, the family seat near Reading in England. This purchase, made in 1977 at about the time the Church was canonizing Bishop John Nepomucene Neumann, the first U.S. male saint, provides an interesting contrast between the two men.

NAPOLEON LED ARMIES across Europe in pomp, circumstance and with martial music. Father John went alone and soundlessly into the wilderness of Western New York State. Napoleon conquered lands and nations: John Neumann looked for people to whom to minister, to bring the Good News of the Gospel.

THE UNIFORM of Napoleon was majestic, gold braided; the cassock of John Neumann was briar-torn, mud-stained and drenched with rain. Both men had greatness in them, each used it differently. Both are remembered and admired. The final question is — which one left a better world for having lived in it?

—ANNE TANSEY

January 6

. . . It is God's will that by doing right you should put to silence the ignorance of foolish men. —1 Peter 2:15

THE three Wise Men from the East are almost at their destination. Yet how little they know about this destination. They carry royal gifts; they find utter poverty. They inquire the way from evil men; unintentionally, they bring on a massacre. How strange their ways! How strange God's ways!

MAINLY THIS IS because we are using, not God's view, but our own. No wonder we get excited over a little success, even though it carries in it the seeds of such failure. No wonder we complain when disappointed, unaware that we are being tested.

"GOD LEADS us by strange ways," wrote Cardinal Newman. "We know He wills our happiness, but we neither know what this happiness is, nor the way . . . we must leave it to Him."

ALL WE ARE really asked to do is what the Wise Men did—get going!

—BISHOP PAUL J. HALLINAN, Charleston, South Carolina

January 7

When they saw the star, they rejoiced exceedingly with great joy; and . . . they saw the child with Mary his mother, and they fell down and worshiped him. Then, opening their treasures, they offered him gifts, gold and frankincense and myrrh. —Matthew 2:10-11

THE Magi, the first-fruits of the Gentile-world, have been admitted into the court of the great King whom they have been seeking, and we have followed them. The Child has smiled on us as He did upon them. All the fatigues of the long journey — which man must take to reach his God — all are over and forgotten; our Emmanuel is with us, and we are with Him.

IN BETHLEHEM, we have the Child, and Mary His Mother. Where else could we find riches like these? Let us beseech this incomparable Mother to give us this Child of hers, our light, our love and our Bread of life, as we approach the altar, led by the star of our faith.

LET US OPEN OUR TREASURES; He will be pleased with our gifts, and we know He never suffers himself to be outdone in generosity. Let us love God, rejoicing that God first loved us, but let us love in deed and in truth.

—BISHOP ANDREW G. GRUTKA, Gary, Indiana

January 8

He who eats my flesh and drinks my blood has eternal life, and I will raise him up at the last day. For my flesh is food indeed, and my blood is drink indeed. —John 6: 54-55

EPIPHANY comes also through the Eucharist. Jesus is shown to the world in the Mass and in Holy Communion. He presents himself daily on thousands of altars to millions of us.

ALL OUR CATHOLIC life pivots around this fact of the Mass: Look at Christ's life for the pattern. He spent the time of His life with His Apostles, teaching, insisting, preparing for the Mass. This was His most important "project," this would last forever, this would give every man of every age His divine presence: the Mass.

ALL IMPORTANT Catholic affairs take place at Mass. Out of it comes our life, our hope, our strength. Each of us has his problems, trying to find our way to God. God gives Himself and the answers to living in the Mass. It is time for us to know it and to live it.

—MSGR. ALEXANDER SIGUR

January 9

. . . The seed is the word of God. —Luke 8:11

NURSERY catalogues begin arriving in the mail as soon as the new year begins. Outside the ground is frozen and snow is falling, but inside gardeners thumb through colorful pages and make new plans for spring gardens.

JESUS LIKENED the kingdom of God to a mustard seed that would grow into a tree in which birds would nest. He indicated that faith is not inactive but goes through stages to great power.

NO SEED remains motionless in a flower pot. It germinates, draws particles of the soil into its composition and structure, imparts to them a higher nature, organizes the sand and makes it living material. It draws upon all the powers of nature. When it is planted outside in the spring it makes use of new soil, sun and rain until it fulfills its destiny—blooms into a beautiful flower, a bush or tree, according to its species.

—ANNE TANSEY

January 10

God also bore witness by signs and wonders and various miracles and by gifts of the Holy Spirit distributed according to his own will.
                                                —Hebrews 2: 4

WE supplement our daily foods with vitamins. The Holy Spirit's vitamins for our souls come through the fruits He offers: charity, or love, joy, peace, patience, kindness, generosity, forbearance, gentleness, faith, courtesy, temperance and purity. These twelve hallmarks attest to the genuine character of a practicing Christian.

WE MIGHT also liken the Holy Spirit to a light switch. God the Father created the electricity. The Son put the system into operation through His act of redemption. Spiritual grace is the flow of electricity within us, but we must come to recognize its indwelling through the Holy Spirit.

IT REQUIRES an act of our will to switch on. Through this willed action the flow of grace circulates in us. Our lives can be Christ-like in daily living and loving.

—MARION EGAN

January 11

. . . Be attentive to my words; incline your ear to my sayings.

—Proverbs 4:20

WE hear the Words of Life at every Mass. These are words to live by! We hear of Christ's compassion on the sick and needy, His dislike of hypocrisy, His warning for those who give scandal. We notice how He gave himself to Jew and Gentile, how there was no caste system or race prejudice in His approach. We hear, and then we act.

WE TRY ourselves to show compassion, to be concerned about our suffering and needy brethren. We try to root up hypocrisy, to avoid all phoniness, to mean what we say. And we examine our conscience, to see if we are unlike Christ in showing dislike to those of another race or color.

THIS IS HOW we live the Gospel part of Mass during the week. The book is closed, the voice of the priest is silent. But our lives are open for all men to see, and our voices speak out, in offices and factories, in homes and neighborhoods. *"Lord, how many men are waiting to hear you! Let me be your voice."*

—FATHER JOSEPH T. NOLAN

January 12

What therefore God has joined together, let no man put asunder. —Matthew 19: 6

THE Scriptures point the way to the kind of married love we are talking about, the kind that Jesus performed His first miracle for.

"Happy is the husband of a good wife, twice lengthened are his days."

"For this reason a man leaves his father and his mother and clings to his wife, and the two become one flesh."

THERE IS more here than meets the eye. Love has brought forth children, and family, a household and a thousand cares and concerns and responsibilities completely unplanned for, and certainly not foreseen. When love has built this kind of a house for itself, and borne the burdens of the years, and is still very much alive when husband and wife look at each other, then this is love truly worthy of the name, and it is this love that God consecrates and the Church celebrates.

—FATHER CLIFFORD STEVENS

January 13

And which of you by being anxious can add a cubit to his span of life? If then you are not able to do as small a thing as that, why are you anxious about the rest? —Luke 12:25-26

AT times, does it seem that no one ever notices you? Like a flower blooming in some cranny of a mountain peak, you are unseen and unappreciated. If this bothers you then let it not.

YOU ARE SEEN and appreciated. Nothing of goodness, truth or beauty ever passes unseen. God who is all goodness, all truth, all beauty, gathers it unto himself and it becomes a part of what is infinitely greater. But even knowing this, it is only natural that you should want some appreciation, want some credit for what good you accomplish in the world.

IF YOU DO NOT get it then remember that God Incarnate, Jesus Christ, lived quietly and unnoticed in the world for thirty years. When men began to see Him as He was, His neighbors back at Nazareth laughed and said, how can He be anything, He's just one of our country boys from Nazareth.

—DALE FRANCIS

January 14

Jesus was led up by the Spirit into the wilderness to be tempted by the devil. And he fasted forty days and forty nights. . . . —Matthew 4:1-2

OVERLOOKING the Jordan valley is the Mount of Temptation where Jesus fasted forty days. This mention of the ascetical life in Matthew's Gospel as something of a prerequisite to Christ's public career was taken as a mandate by St. Anthony and the early desert monks.

THE INTERIOR life is still incumbent upon the apostolic Christian. It only seems to have gone out of style. The desert fathers say the apostolate can only be an overflow of an interior bounty; otherwise active works are fruitless.

I ASKED a busy Holy Land priest how he managed to earn his wide reputation for achievement, availability, and readiness to cope with the unexpected. He modestly disclaimed such a reputation, saying only: "Out of my weakness and shallowness, I must deliberately set aside large amounts of time for recollection and, mysteriously, I get more done that way."

—MSGR. JOHN G. NOLAN

January 15

Whatever was written in former days was written for our instruction, that by steadfastness and by the encouragement of the scriptures we might have hope. —Romans 15:4

OUR Blessed Lady was not a priest nor bishop. Queen of the Clergy that she is, she did not forgive sins nor celebrate Mass. But she was surely the Church's ideal parishioner!

CONCERNED over the embarrassed couple at Cana, she was considerate. Hurrying to help her cousin Elizabeth, she was compassionate. In the Acts of the Apostles, we find one line describing her in that first apostolic parish: "The Apostles with one mind continued steadfastly in prayer with the women, and Mary the Mother of Jesus." This harmony of solid public prayer and gentle unobtrusive kindness, we must seek. Mary did not stop at private prayer to her Lord. In the first "lay participation," she joined with all the rest in "the communion of the breaking of the bread and in the prayers."

—BISHOP PAUL J. HALLINAN, Charleston, South Carolina

January 16

Let your light so shine before men, that they may see your good works and give glory to your Father who is in heaven.
—Matthew 5:16

LIGHT serves as a key symbol in the baptismal ceremony as it does throughout the New Testament. We are given a light at baptism, drawn from the Easter candle, that great symbol of Christ in our midst. Our light, we are told, is to shine out before others as we journey through life.

HOW CLEAR were the words of Jesus when He proclaimed from the mountaintop: "Do not hide your lights under bushel baskets!" Yet how difficult His command becomes as we really try to live it. How easy it is to let our lights shine at Sunday Mass. How hard it is to carry that light to the office with us Monday morning or to that sick (and always complaining) friend whom we know we should visit, but. . . .

A SMALL, single candle can light an entire room, breaking the grip of darkness and fear, giving us just enough of a glow to see our way around and know where we are.

—JAMES MICHAEL SULLIVAN

January 17

If any one thinks he is something, when he is nothing, he deceives himself. —Galatians 6:3

D O your own thing is the presently popular phrase. It's probably a reflection of the advice "Be yourself" that we were told, or "Know yourself" as the philosopher commanded. In any case, it tells us to face up to the realities of our own potential in day-to-day living.

FREEDOM is a God-given gift and as such it is most precious. Whenever law or authority tries to restrict the exercise of our liberty, we have the right to know the exact basis of the prohibition. Unless the common good is obviously at stake, we also have the right to question the authority involved.

ON THE other hand, the golden virtue of charity will most often guide us in restricting our own freedom. The virtue which St. Thomas Aquinas considers as basic — justice, will also help us to govern our liberty. It's challenging to "do our own thing," as long as it doesn't make us selfish along the way.

—FATHER CHARLES DOLLEN

January 18

With thee is the fountain of life; in thy light do we see light.
—Psalms 36:9

M Y life is necessarily filled with successes and failures. Usually I am elated by success and discouraged by failure. Yet neither one should make any difference. Success is empty, even among the most brilliant. And when I rest in it, I begin to get a false sense of my own value. Failure doesn't say anything about me, even though it may seem to say something to my friends and my critics. Some people will rejoice in my failures as almost a success of their own; to me it should simply free me from a few illusions.

THE CHRISTIAN does his task in this world. He puts his hand to the plow and plows the furrow God has designated for him. But his eyes are on the homeland. If this seems too idealistic and difficult, if the labor of providing food for the stomach, shelter over my head and clothes for my back seems to be all-absorbing, I had better stop short and ask myself a few questions. In a hundred years I will be dead, it will be all over; the body I am taking so much trouble to feed and clothe and shelter will long be in the grave. But my soul? And my place before God? Maybe I should take time to nourish my spirit.

—FATHER BLASE SCHAUER, O.P.

January 19

Have no anxiety about anything, but in everything by prayer and supplication with thanksgiving let your requests be made known to God. —Philippians 4:6

DAILY meditation is a good thing — a time alone with God — but it is not the whole day. What can I do during all the busy hours to stay close to His grace? Every time I feel confused or hurried I pause, for just a moment, and think of God or look for His guidance.

WHEN A STRANGER knocks at the door or a phone call interrupts what I am doing — even prayer — I try to respond with love. I know that God controls all things except my free will. If I am angry or hurt or confused or anxious it is because *I* am blocking *His* abiding grace. God never fails to respond to a thought, a prayer or an act done in love.

OH GOD I know you are here within me and within every person and moment I meet. The joys I feel, the beauty I see, the love I give is Your grace within me. Help me to keep tuned in that I may be Thy willing instrument.

—BETTY WICKHAM

January 20

. . . Make every effort to supplement your faith with virtue, and virtue with knowledge. . . . —2 Peter 1:5

NO doubt about it, the best goal we can set in life is striving for virtue. It is important that we do not let the matter depend upon chance or the mood of the moment. Let us rather select a definite virtue toward which we are going to bend every effort.

FROM our frequent confession we ought to have some idea of what our predominant fault is. That is the fault we have to include in just about every confession we make. Once we have established this, we plan our attack.

SELECT the opposite corresponding virtue. For example, if impurity is our predominant fault, we select purity as the corresponding virtue. This now becomes the focal point of interest. We marshal our forces not so much to avoid impurity but rather to acquire purity. In this way, we are accentuating the positive. We begin to see our relationship with God is not one of "don'ts" but one of "do's."

—FATHER ALBERT J. NIMETH, O.F.M.

January 21

Sing praises to the Lord, O you his saints. . . . —Psalms 30:4

WHO are all these saints mentioned in the Canon of the Mass? They are a wonderfully mixed-up crowd. The Apostles are there, and so are the first successors to Peter as Bishops of Rome (Linus, Cletus, Clement, Xystus, etc.). But all these names in the Canon are not just priests and clergy. John and Paul were in the Roman army. Cosmas and Damian were physicians. Felicitas was a wealthy young Roman matron. Perpetua was her slave girl, and they were both mothers.

THERE IS ALSO a husband and wife who are mentioned, named Joseph and Mary!

ALL THIS VARIETY reminds us that there are many walks and ways to serve God. The carpenter and the soldier, the physician and his housewife, the rich young lady and the serving girl, then or now, are equally dear in the sight of God. And they all have the calling to serve Him, to be saints.

—FATHER JOSEPH T. NOLAN

January 22

The angel Gabriel came to Mary and said, "Hail, full of grace, the Lord is with you!" —Luke 1:28

THE speaker was eloquently denouncing all those who were trying to "downgrade Mary." A woman in the audience asked, "How would it be possible for any mere human to take from or add to what Mary was — the mother of Jesus Christ?"

THE CONTROVERSY over Mary which has arisen during the post-Conciliar period is actually one of varied "images" by which she is viewed by Catholic people. There are some who cannot see her in any other manner but as a "Queen." Others see her as she appeared at Lourdes, Fatima, Guadalupe, Pontmain, LaSalette, and so on.

NO MATTER by how many different titles she is known, Mary was only one person, a Jewish woman who gave birth to Jesus Christ, the Redeemer of mankind. This was certainly the greatest height to which a woman could be called. No other fact can dwarf this one, that Mary brought our Redeemer into the world.

—ANNE TANSEY

January 23

You, therefore, must be perfect, as your heavenly Father is perfect.
—Matthew 5:48

C HRIST came on earth to teach us by word and example how to live in order to merit eternal salvation. In His exhortations He pleaded that we become perfect — as perfect as the Heavenly Father. In other words Christ wants us to be God-like.

THIS IS A BIG goal to strive for and one that requires the help of Heaven itself. This help is available if sought after sincerely.

THERE ARE some qualities of God that we can imitate quite readily and most effectively. These qualities are meekness, kindness, mercy and compassion. Try practicing these qualities and experience for yourself how much good can be accomplished and how readily the warmth of the light of Christ can be reflected through your own personality.

—BISHOP ANDREW G. GRUTKA, Gary, Indiana

January 24

. . . The fruit of the Spirit is love, joy, peace, patience, kindness, goodness, faithfulness, gentleness. . . . —Galatians 5:22-23

S T. Francis de Sales was a gentle man. The doctor of gentleness, but not the kind of gentleness which says "Yes" to everything, which is afraid to be forceful in Faith for fear of offending, or is kind to enemies and critics to avoid a fight. St. Francis de Sales was a fighter, and as a young man had been the finest swordsman at the university. But he had a naturally fiery temper and he worked to conquer that. He ended up in becoming a most gentle man, but a man forceful in the ways that really counted.

TO TURN the other cheek does not mean that we must let people push us around, trample on our rights and oppress us to take advantage of us. We do not have to let ourselves become the victims of parasites, bores and imperious people. Rather, there is a much deeper truth here. What Our Lord is saying in that remarkable statement is that we must learn to enrich even those people who don't enrich us. That we must be bigger than any situation we find ourselves in, and that we must not be so petty that we can't take an inconvenience. We have to learn, not to take it, but to give it; to give of ourselves, to live in a world larger than the world around us, and to walk in this world as if we were not here.

—FATHER BLASE SCHAUER, O.P.

January 25

Give thanks to the Lord, call upon his name; make known his deeds among the nations. . . . —Isaiah 12:4

WHEN John F. Noll was born, on Jan. 25, 1875, who could have foretold the profound influence he was to have on the Church in America. He grew up at a time when virulent anti-Catholicism was rampant in the land.

HE TURNED to the Catholic press to tell the truth about our Church. Later, he was made Bishop of Fort Wayne, Indiana. His work, as we know it, still continues in the *Our Sunday Visitor* family of papers, magazines, books and related materials. He was also a co-founder of the Catholic Press Association.

BISHOP NOLL'S work was to spread the good news about Christ and His Church in the English-speaking world. That should be our mission, too. Have you invited anyone to Mass, recently? Have you asked anyone if he or she wants to learn more about this dynamic Church?

—FATHER CHARLES DOLLEN

January 26

The Lord said to Paul one night in a vision, "Do not be afraid, but speak and do not be silent; for I am with you. . . ." —Acts 18:9

ST. Paul is the perfect model of those who never look back. From the first flash of lightning that threw him to the ground outside Damascus to the moment when the executioner's ax flashed above his head, he was the total Christian, and he never looked back even for a moment. It is true that there were many forward steps that he took and that the Christian vision grew with the years; he found totally unsuspected facets in his Faith that he poured into his marvelous epistles, but he never swerved from that complete and undivided loyalty to Christ that marked his conversion.

WE OFTEN think that the age of such heroes is over, or that the kind of fire and conviction that St. Paul showed is simply not for us. But God never changes and neither does Christ; in our own way we have to be Paul; we have to burn with a fire; we have to shed around us a light that will enlighten others. We cannot escape from the inevitable consequences of our Faith, as St. Paul could not. But for that to happen perhaps we need the equivalent of his three years in the Arabian desert.

—FATHER BLASE SCHAUER, O.P.

January 27

Tend the flock of God that is your charge, not by constraint but willingly, not for shameful gain but eagerly, not as domineering over those in your charge but being examples to the flock. —I Peter 5:2

YEARS ago we visited an out-state parish whose pastor stood at the church door greeting each person after Mass. In the case of ourselves, he welcomed us as visitors, asked our Christian names, and in the course of perhaps five sentences repeated our names three times.

MONTHS LATER we returned to this church. Father V. recalled our names by the magic of the triple-repetition the first time. We felt warmed and enfolded. This priest's practice of courtesy directed him to identify each sheep of the flock and note the strays.

NOT ALL priests are aware of the importance of public relations. Parishioners can help by making visitors feel part of the family of God through the practice of this fruit of the Holy Spirit.

—MARION EGAN

January 28

Behold, God is my salvation; I will trust, and will not be afraid; for the Lord God is my strength and my song. . . . — Isaiah 12:2

THERE is something about St. Thomas Aquinas — this most inaccessible of saints — that makes him a unique model of holiness. A fellow Dominican, Father Thomas Deman, wrote of him: "Among all possible objects St. Thomas chose to know God. We can bring back to that one point the accumulation of knowledge he carried in his mind. . . . In the sphere of the intellect, St. Thomas had become a kind of companion of God. He kept to his solitude to live habitually in such company."

THIS DEEP contemplative spirit that makes a person a true companion of God in this life is rare in the present age. "By loving God," St. Thomas himself writes, "we glow to gaze on His beauty." The study of God was the one passion of his life and even as a boy of seven he asked his teachers the question: "What is God?" He spent his whole life trying to find the answer.

EACH ONE of us has to learn to seek God in the tangle of our minds, trying to catch glimpses of His greatness as we grapple with His Truth.

—FATHER CLIFFORD STEVENS

January 29

Can mortal man be righteous before God? Can a man be pure before his Maker? —Job 4:17

ONE of the first things we learned about a sacrament is that it is an "outward sign." Every Christian is called to be a sacrament, an outward sign, formed in the love of Christ, to be a communicator of God's grace to others.

THESE ARE our sacraments. Our Church has formalized them into seven, building on our human graces which naturally focus on times and events which hallmark our development. It is not coincidence that birthdays and anniversaries are central to our lives.

THE CHURCH, through Christ, the great sacrament, is with us more than once or twice a year. Christ is with us in a special sacramental way at every key point in our lives. He welcomes us at baptism and confirms us at the beginning of our maturity. He reconciles us in failure and unites us to himself and to each other in Eucharist. He calls us to leadership in His community or to the formation of families within that community. He is there as we risk the loss of our earthly lives, stretching toward us as we make our final struggle toward His eternal life.

—JAMES MICHAEL SULLIVAN

January 30

Lead me, O Lord, in thy righteousness . . . make the way straight before me. —Psalms 5:8

GOD'S man lives, moves, has his being in God. The Christian who would live godly always must have a rule or pattern of life. Here is a suggestion:

• Participate daily in the Holy Sacrifice. Everything — work, play, prayer — shares in it: *Ite Missa Est.*

• Feast daily on the Eucharist — Christ is your great Friend — take Him with you.

• Make daily conversation with Christ — mental prayer — aim for 15 minutes, settle for no less than five, on busiest days.

• Receive the Sacrament of Penance biweekly, with a regular confessor if possible. Seek spiritual direction.

• Pray Our Lady's Rosary daily, devoutly.

• Use opportunities to increase knowledge of our Holy Faith: courses, lectures, discussion clubs, books, sermons.

—MSGR. ALEXANDER SIGUR

January 31

Is there a thing of which it is said, "See, this is new"? It has been already, in the ages before us. —Ecclesiastes 1:10

JANUARY is the kind of month in which the spirit can grow. The voice of God is more audible in the frozen silence. Things are going on in the underearth of society as well as in the land.

THE IDEALS OF GOD are often lost in the lushness of summer. But the counterculture which is making itself visible in human society is stirring its own seeds to challenge those of the seeds of materialism, apathy and indifference which have run over the garden of man for too many decades. This counterculture, with its new value system, is cutting across income and age, sex and situation in life. It places more emphasis on friendship, the quality of life, and the inherent needs of all, rather than how well each will "make it" economically. Everything bigger is not better. Success is relative. Actually what is it?

THE CULTURE which Jesus brought to the world can come alive again in gentle things, in people, caring, sharing. Its echoes are already in the ears of the sensitive. One day it will become manifest in action, just as spring will become a reality when winter passes.

—ANNE TANSEY

February 1

. . . The steadfast love is before my eyes, and I walk in faithfulness to thee. —Psalms 26:3

"HOW beautiful a day can be when kindness touches it!" This thought I found printed on the envelope of a recent letter. It impressed me. It is simple yet lovely.

ONE THING that keeps many of us from being better Christians is our much too idealistic idea of a Christ-follower. We feel that to be a real Christian one must do great and heroic things, when in actuality all Christ wants from us is a little more kindness to our neighbor. We realize soon that we cannot be great saints — so we end up doing nothing. The devil encourages us to think this way.

WE ARE little people. We must be humble and realistic enough to realize this. We can do only little things, but Christ expects us to do that. Try a little kindness.

—FATHER RAWLEY MYERS

February 2

When the time came for their purification according to the law of Moses, they brought him up to Jerusalem to present him to the Lord. —Luke 2:22

JOSEPH and Mary have come to offer their Son to the Lord. Simeon takes the infant from their hands and utters the prophecy that rings through the centuries: "This child is destined to be the downfall and rise of many in Israel, a sign that will be opposed." He will be a sign of contradiction, says Simeon. And over and over again his words prove true.

JESUS and His Gospel stand in constant opposition to the values of a world without faith in God or moral values. His warnings against love of money, comfort and pleasure contradict the values of people seeking happiness in things and possessions. His call to sacrifice, to care for the poor and to renounce violence "accuses" the self-centered and self-seeking. His call to chastity, purity, fidelity convict those who promote open marriage, premarital sex, etc.

PRAYER: Jesus, help me see in You and the cross a constant challenge to my own values and goals in life. Grant that my life, like Yours, may also become a sign in opposition to those who reject You and the cross.

—FATHER NORMAN PERRY, O.F.M.

February 3

The path of the righteous is like the light of dawn, which shines brighter and brighter until full day. —Proverbs 4:18

I am going to reveal to you a secret of sanctity and happiness. If every day during five minutes, you will keep your imagination quiet, shut your eyes to all the things of sense, and close your ears to all the sound of earth, so as to be able to withdraw into the sanctuary of your baptized soul, which is the temple of the Holy Spirit, speaking there to that Holy Spirit, saying: "O Holy Spirit, soul of my soul, I adore Thee. Enlighten, guide, strengthen and console me. Tell me what I ought to do and command me to do it. I promise to be submissive in everything that You permit to happen to me, only show me what is Thy will."

IF YOU DO this, your life will pass happily and serenely. Consolation will abound even in the midst of troubles. Grace will be given in proportion to the trial as well as strength to bear it, bringing you to the Gates of Paradise full of merit. This submission to the Holy Spirit is the Secret of Sanctity. — (*Cardinal Mercier*)
—BISHOP LEO A. PURSLEY, Fort Wayne-South Bend, Indiana

February 4

All of you, have unity of spirit, sympathy, love of the brethren, a tender heart and a humble mind. —I Peter 3:8

THERE is nothing more alien to the Christian spirit than boredom. This feeling is more subtle than sin, of which it is the seed. It can find an easy entrance into us where sin cannot. If it is not rooted out, it will yield a harvest of sin. Boredom leads us to keep our distance from the tasks which are crying for attention in the Church. It shows us how to be hypersensitive about our personal rights and prestige. It makes us forget that our liberty increases by solidarity with common problems and that in the Gospel's perspective God's rights always have priority over our own.

NO ONE was less bored than St. Paul. He who spoke most about the Christian's participation in Christ's passion is also the New Testament author who has left the best description of Christian joy.
—FATHER ROMAN GINN, O.C.S.O.

February 5

"He that would love life and see good days, let him keep his tongue from evil and his lips from speaking guile. . . ." —1 Peter 3:10

AUTOMOBILE travelers and workers in offices face constant irritations each day. Housewives and factory workers have their share of upset plans as well. Each of us finds some humiliation in our path no matter how talented we may be in forestalling mishaps. Yet we never have sufficient reason to grumble at inconvenience, since none of us loves God as well as we might. So why do we fret at the little trials He might send us?

THE PURPOSE of every trial is to enable us to love Him better, to withdraw just a bit more from the allurements of the world which knows Him not.

OUR BLESSED MOTHER lived every day of her life perfectly. God was delighted with her. And yet He did not spare her many fearful trials. Could you have borne the cross of knowing that you had lost Jesus for three days? Could you have stood, while He writhed in agony on His own cross? If Mary was sent these trials to intensify her love for God, then let us welcome our own trials with open arms, as the saints have done.

—FATHER DONALD F. X. CONNOLLY

February 6

Yet if one suffers as a Christian, let him not be ashamed, but under that name let him glorify God. —I Peter 4:16

SAINT Paul Miki and 25 companions were crucified at Nagasaki, Japan, in the 16th century for their faith in Christ.

HOW OFTEN do we today express thanks to God that we live in a country where a man is not persecuted or martyred for his faith? And how often do we pray for the many in Communist countries this very minute who are suffering because they follow Christ? We American Christians are so comfortable we take our gifts for granted, and we think that everyone enjoys the liberty we have here.

AMERICANS have been so blessed. We live in one of the great garden spots of the world. A pure gift of God to us; we just happened — in His wonderful Providence — to be born here. And we enjoy in this land a freedom that few people in the world know.

—FATHER RAWLEY MYERS

February 7

Of making many books there is no end. . . . —Ecclesiastes 12:12

NOW we are getting to the point of talking about things we ought to do in order to be what we were created to be, and in order to make a tremendous, unending success of our lives.

FOR INSTANCE, we ought to do some good reading. Not a great deal, necessarily. If we will read for one minute a day about Christ in the Gospels, and then think, we will make amazing progress. The simple fact is that we can't care about what we don't know about, and we can't care much about what we don't know much about, and don't think about. That is why good reading is important.

CHRIST CAME, Truth Himself, to give us truth — but we've got to let Him get through to us. He left us the Gospels so that we could hear what He had to say to us, just as if we had been with Him in the Holy Land. We will be surprised how our taste for His truth will grow if only we will savor it each day.

—JOSEPH A. BREIG

February 8

I say this not as a command, but to prove by the earnestness of others that your love is also genuine. —2 Corinthians 8:8

AN old Roman source tells us that when skillfully hand-carved statues were transported in ancient times they sometimes suffered in the process minor injuries — chipping. To sell their wares at full price, the dealers had a way of "touching up" the damaged spots with wax — a finger, a toe, a nose. Customers eventually discovered this, and it became customary for a prospective buyer to ask, *"Sine cera?"* (Without wax?)

WE HAVE come to use the word "sincere" from that background. "Sincere" means that the whole is genuine; no part is (like wax) a make-believe substitute.

SINCERITY is a much desired quality. We trust and believe the sincere person; we doubt the word of the hypocrite. However, it just may be that sometimes we ourselves are guilty of patching a "bad looking" spot with a substitute.

LORD, melt away my wax patches with Your Love, for You are The Truth, sincere to the core!

—THERESITA POLZIN

February 9

. . . The man of haughty looks and arrogant heart I will not endure. —Psalms 101:5

THE only real way to become a saint is to avoid letting anyone know that you are one. To hear men talk about themselves, everyone is a king or a boss or a millionaire. Nobody ever admits that he is just another leaf on the tree. That is being humble.

IT IS ONLY too bad that we must persist in treading bubble trails through the clouds. It is only too bad that we cannot come down and walk the earth like true, humble men.

THE MAN who sets himself too tall in the saddle tends to look down. And the man who always looks down never sees the stars. So in missing the stars, he misses the perfect work of the only person who is able to proclaim himself perfect.

A PROUD MAN bemoans the fact that he must live in the midst of so many inferior beings. Let him take consolation in the fact that if he cannot find his equal on earth, he will certainly find his equal in hell.

—FATHER RICHARD MADDEN, O.C.D.

February 10

The tongue of the wise dispenses knowledge, but the mouths of fools pour out folly. —Proverbs 15:2

"GLIB" is a word that describes a great deal of religious talk. Often, a person who talks thoughtfully on many subjects falls into cliché. He repeats pious words that have lost their meaning — when he talks about religion and God.

ST. SCHOLASTICA, whose feast we celebrate today, was a sister of Saint Benedict and consecrated her life to God when very young. Later she founded and governed a convent of nuns. Separated from her brother by responsibilities, frequent meetings were not possible. They did meet, however, once a year, and their conversation would be about spiritual matters.

IT IS GOOD to avoid empty talk, and dishonest talk. As Thomas à Kempis said, "We must watch and pray, lest our time pass away idly." The same applies to conversation. While you talk about this you can't talk about that. If possible, talk with someone about God. Let conversation be honest and humble.

—DONALD F. CROWHURST

February 11

Blessed is she who believed that there would be a fulfillment of what was spoken to her from the Lord. —Luke 1:45

IN 1854, Pope Pius IX solemnly proclaimed to the world that Mary is the Immaculate Conception. The doctrine which holds that she was never for an instant contaminated by the infection of Original Sin has been believed by the Church from the beginning and must be accepted as a dogma.

ON FEBRUARY 11, 1858, a little French girl named Bernadette Soubirous who lived in a small town nestled in the Pyrenees mountains was gathering firewood at some distance from her home when she was suddenly startled by the appearance of a glorious Lady in a cleft of rock: pure white gown and mantle with an azure blue girdle and holding a rosary! Later, March 25, the Lady announced her name: "I am the Immaculate Conception," she said.

DURING the century, millions have gone to Lourdes: there have been thousands of cures, but the great miracle is a miracle of faith and love. Today is the feast of Our Lady of Lourdes.

—FATHER JOHN C. SELNER, S.S.

February 12

When a man's ways please the Lord, he makes even his enemies to be at peace with him. —Proverbs 16:7

"I am not bound to win," wrote Abraham Lincoln, "but I am bound to be true. I am not bound to succeed, but I am bound to live by the light that I have. I must stand with anybody that stands right, stand with him while he is right, and part with him when he goes wrong."

THE LINE between arrogance and integrity is sometimes hard to see, but we have to have a firm guiding principle in our conflicts with other people. We cannot avoid conflict, but we can avoid the meanness sometimes associated with conflict and the human respect that is afraid to be lowered in the esteem of others.

AGAIN, Abraham Lincoln expresses this nicely: "With malice towards none, with charity for all, with firmness in the right as God gives us to see the right." Or, in the words of St. Thomas Aquinas: "Lord God, grant that when I fight for love of truth, I may not lose the truth of love."

—FATHER CLIFFORD STEVENS

February 13

Jesus said: "Woman, behold, your son!" —John 19:26

THE multitude departed; Calvary is left solitary and still, except that Saint John and the holy women are there. Then came Joseph of Arimathea and Nicodemus, to take down from the cross the body of Jesus, and place it in the arms of Mary.

O MARY, at last you have possession of your Son. Now, when His enemies can do no more, they leave Him to you. Your heart is pierced with the sword of which Simeon spoke. Without swooning, without trembling, you receive Him. Now you are supremely happy, though He comes to you not as He went forth from you. He went from your home in the strength and beauty of His manhood, and He comes back dislocated, torn to pieces, mangled, dead.

YET, O Blessed Mary, you are happier in this hour than on the day of the marriage feast, for then He was leaving you and now and in the future as the Risen Savior, He will be separated from you no more.

—FATHER WILFRED ILLIES

February 14

. . . Declare thy steadfast love in the morning, and thy faithfulness by night, to the music of the lute and the harp. . . . —Psalms 92:2-3

CHAUCER really started the whole thing. It is he who tells us that the birds take their mates on Valentine's Day and who are we to dispute so delightful and ancient an author? Of course, Alban Butler says that ancient Rome had a pagan love festival in mid-February so St. Valentine's Day observances were chosen as a substitute.

TAKE YOUR PICK of these reasons, but send your Valentines anyway. In *Ready or Not* (Boston, St. Paul Editions) I tell the teenagers that it is a wholesome practice to express love in varying degrees to many people. So often feelings get hurt because no one notices the good we do. (They seldom miss our mistakes!) So often husbands do not show the appreciation and love that they have for their wives. Can any woman be told too often that she is loved?

I FREQUENTLY wonder why so many flowers are sent to funerals. Wouldn't these expressions of love have been much more appreciated if they had been sent to the person while living?

—FATHER CHARLES DOLLEN

February 15

And whatever you ask in prayer, you will receive, if you have faith.
—Matthew 21:22

PRAYER does not make suffering any more bearable but it does help us to understand that it has a relationship to our eternal life. We can endure suffering when our faith gives us the hope to know "why" someday.

WE CANNOT call upon faith, however, unless we have developed its strength and intelligence with prayer. Faith does not come from will power but as a gift in response to our deep relationship with God. We cannot create faith when we need it. We must already have it and prayer keeps it fresh and vibrant.

PRAYER does not necessarily give answers but it does give direction. It also offers a good fusion point for our ideas and feelings to meet and settle differences. Prayer settles the mind and emotions by quieting the spirit and then proceeds to overcome our anxieties by refreshing our faith, assuring forgiveness and convincing us of our sacred dignity before God.

—FATHER JOHN C. TORMEY

February 16

We see Jesus, who for a little while was made lower than the angels, crowned with glory and honor because of the suffering of death, so that by the grace of God he might taste death for everyone. —Hebrews 2:9

SUFFERING escapes no one. Worldwide, men, women and children are not spared from the agony or the anguish of suffering. Though it is difficult to bear for many, suffering is a test of faithfulness. It is the road to perfection and union with Christ.

FAITH and love of God reflect our reaction to suffering. Some fear it, intensely. They try to evade it, often in vain. Others welcome it with a smile as the bearer of grace. For some, suffering is sterile. To others, it is dangerous. Still to others, suffering makes atonement and merits redemption.

WE MUST know how to accept suffering. Christ teaches us how to bear it, how to carry our cross. He, Who has a great heart, Who died on the Cross after so much agony and suffering, and He alone can teach us through His own great sorrow because He loved mankind enough to suffer so much for us.

—MARIE LAYNE

February 17

Mary said, "Behold, I am the handmaid of the Lord; let it be to me according to your word." —Luke 1:38

H OW many memories must suddenly come back to You, my dear Savior, as You meet Your mother on the way of the cross. Memories of Your infancy, when she held You in her arms, memories of Your youth, when she made Your poor home rich with her love; memories of her loyalty, who never hurt You by a fault or sin! But now she can only gaze on You as You pass by, Your face clotted with blood and sweat, Your body bent and staggering, Your heart stung by blasphemy and insult!

YET THIS meeting was meant to atone for my sins against my loved ones. How often I failed my family by disobedience to my parents; by quarreling with a brother or sister; by carrying grudges and showing resentment when I was crossed!

O MARY, perfect mother of a perfect Son, teach me in your way of unselfish love.

—FATHER DONALD F. MILLER, C.SS.R.

February 18

. . . My spirit rejoices in God my Savior, for he has regarded the low estate of his handmaiden. For behold, henceforth all generations will call me blessed. . . . —Luke 1:47-48

P OPE PAUL VI, at the closing of the third session of Vatican II, (November 21, 1964) proclaimed: "For the glory of the Virgin Mary and for our own consolation, we proclaim the Most Blessed Virgin Mary Mother of the Church, that is to say of all the People of God, of the faithful as well as of the pastors, who call her the most loving Mother.

"WE DESIRE that the Mother of God should be still more honored and invoked by the entire Christian people by this most sweet title.

"O MARY, to your Immaculate Heart we recommend the entire human race. Lead it to the knowledge of the sole and true Savior, Jesus Christ. Protect it from the scourges provoked by sin, give to the entire world peace, in truth, in justice, in liberty and in love." Mary, Help of Christians, pray for us.

—FATHER PASCHAL BOLAND, O.S.B.

February 19

Pleasant words are like a honeycomb, sweetness to the soul and health to the body. —Proverbs 16:24

THE message received is not always the message sent. We often second-guess or prejudge a message before we receive it. Misunderstanding is the natural consequence.

WE MISUNDERSTAND because we do not listen. We hear. But understanding is more than a physical vibration of the eardrum. Listening places the message in the context of the conversation and patiently waits for the opportunity to clarify and assimilate.

ONCE ASSIMILATED, intelligence digests its meaning and prudently responds to the total expression of the message sent. Without this process of reception, communication does not have a chance. Frank Sheed says, "In marriage reverence is more important than love."

—FATHER JOHN C. TORMEY

February 20

He who oppresses a poor man insults his Maker, but he who is kind to the needy honors him. —Proverbs 14:31

WE must be patient and understanding with those around us. We must suspend judgment on their actions. We won't know the whole story on their motives until Judgment Day. If we could know now, it's very likely we'd understand and forgive. "He forgives all who knows all," the French say.

THE EASIEST, the simplest shortcut is this: Accustom yourself to seeing God in everyone you meet. Treat everybody as Christ treats you. When a demand is put on you for something — a handout, a service of any sort — consider it as Our Lord making the request and be happy that you are privileged to serve Him in disguise.

DON'T RAIL at Him and scold. Be generous. Be patient. He comes to us in many a guise and shape, but we must never fail to recognize Him and to say, with the child Samuel, "Speak, Lord, for Thy servant hears you."

—VOL. 1, NO. 1/MDV/FEB. 1957

February 21

The man called his wife's name Eve, because she was the mother of all living. —Genesis 3:20

IT is almost impossible for us to celebrate any feast of Our Lady without being grateful to her for being such a loving mother to us. It is also a good time to check ourselves on our gratitude to our earthly mothers (or even fathers for that matter).

OUR PARENTS are pretty much responsible for everything we have and are. Throughout the course of a lifetime, they provided for our needs, watched through the night when we were sick, and suffered broken hearts at many of our indiscreet capers.

WE OWE our parents all the love we can muster, which should not be difficult for us. We owe them respect, and it doesn't matter how much money they have, or what kind of clothes they wear. They are our parents and nothing else counts.

GOD ONLY gave them to us on loan. When their work is done, God will call them back. So let's treasure them while we have them.
—FATHER RICHARD MADDEN, O.C.D.

February 22

Arise, O Lord! Let not man prevail; let the nations be judged before thee! Put them in fear, O Lord! Let the nations know that they are but men! —Psalms 9:19-20

THE birthday of George Washington can stir up within us a few thoughts on love for country; in many ways that love has a religious foundation, or it should have. If our country is loyal to God it is a good country; if not, then none of its achievements are worth noting.

THE FAMOUS remark by Stephen Decatur "My country: may she always be right; but right or wrong — my country," sounds very impressive, but it is quite misleading. At least it is easily misinterpreted. True patriotism must find its proper level in our country's being right. When it is wrong, some of the blame falls on each of us. We are thinking of right and wrong in the moral sense — not in the sense of political blunders and mistakes.

OUR TRUE union as fellow-countrymen is under God. If we are loyal to His commands, as a nation, we are united and free; if we are not, the true patriot will never rest until we become so.
—FATHER JOHN C. SELNER, S.S.

February 23

Let marriage be held in honor among all . . . —Hebrews 13:4

NOT nearly enough thought has been given to marriage as a vocation. We think of it romantically, and that is all right — romantic it is, and ought to be. But it is also a great vocation. Like everything else, its central purpose is service of God.

GOD COULD people the earth, if He chose, without anybody's instrumentality. He does not so choose. He wills to create His immortal human beings through other human beings united in the institution and the sacrament of marriage. Men and women who see themselves as God's images, made for God's work, must ask in prayer for guidance.

AM I CALLED to marriage? Is that the way of life in which I will best attain my perfection? If so, where is my partner? Who is the soul for whom I was made, and who was made for me?

IN SUCH an approach, in such courageous and open-minded realism, lies the secret of the kind of joyous marriages the world needs.

—JOSEPH A. BREIG

February 24

Blessed is the man who endures trial, for when he has stood the test he will receive the crown of life which God has promised to those who love him. —James 1:12

IT is hundreds and hundreds of years since Moses brought Israel out of Egypt. Hundreds of years since David won glory for Israel. Over and over again Israel has failed Yahweh, abandoned Him to follow false gods, and sought its happiness in the things of the earth. Again and again God has invited Israel to penance and reconciliation. Often Israel has heard the call only to fall away again.

OUR STORY is the same as Israel's. Grace upon grace. Failure upon failure. So many Lents, so many invitations to penance and reconciliation. So often the call half-heartedly answered only to walk away again to look for happiness in the things that have failed us in the past.

PRAYER: Thank You, Lord, for this new opportunity of grace. I want to accept it. Help me once and for all to turn to You and live in Your love and friendship.

—FATHER NORMAN PERRY, O.F.M.

February 25

If a man has a hundred sheep, and one of them has gone astray, does he not leave the ninety-nine on the hills and go in search of the one that went astray? And if he finds it . . . he rejoices over it more than over the ninety-nine that never went astray.

—Matthew 18:12-13

A priest asked a class of boys who it was that was sorrowful and sad when the Prodigal returned. The answer should have been, "The elder brother." A lad, however, returned an answer that gave the world another schoolboy howler. "Please," he said, "it was the fatted calf."

WE CAN'T admire the prodigal son, who, in effect, said to his father, "Give me now a portion of the estate that will be mine anyway when you are dead." He lived a dissolute life but later came to himself and admitted to his father, "I have sinned against God and against you." There is hope for a man like that. But the other son was sorry his brother had returned. In his attitude we observe jealousy, anger, pride, lack of love, cruelty, self-righteousness.

WE DON'T excuse the prodigal son's sins of the flesh. Even as we tend to ignore the elder brother in the story, we ignore the sins of the spirit in ourselves.

—DONALD F. CROWHURST

February 26

. . . Lord; we are perishing. And he said to them, "Why are you afraid, O men of little faith?" —Matthew 8:25-26

"O Lord, set me free from the enslavement of fear."

THIS BEAUTIFUL brief prayer was uttered by a Russian Archbishop. And it says a great deal. Fear dominates the lives of many people. But fear can be conquered by love. And so we should pray that God's love will more and more enter our hearts. With Christ and His love in our hearts we have no room for fear. We trust God, as Our Lord trusted Him. We know that God, our heavenly Father, will see us through.

ONE FILLED with fear sits in the shadows, but if we trust God we walk in the sunshine. Christ says to us: "I am ready to die for you: I love you." With such love for us, why are we fearful? O, we of little faith.

—FATHER RAWLEY MYERS

February 27

Praise God in his sanctuary; praise him in his mighty firmament!
—Psalms 150:1

LITTLE drops of water, little grains of sand, make the mighty ocean and the pleasant land. This little saying, simple in expression, is profound in content. It points out the very important truth that the small efforts and contributions to society by individuals are not to be despised because they are small. The individual labors and combined efforts of all citizens have resulted in the formation of the great nation to which we all give allegiance.

ANOTHER SAYING, "perfection is no trifle, but perfection is made of trifles," emphasizes the same truth in the supernatural sphere. No small act of virtue, no slight denial or mortification is to be considered trifling, since these single actions help establish habits of goodness that form good strong characters.

THIS TRUTH should be pressed deeply upon our minds so that we will never again remain indifferent to the opportunities of performing small deeds that will lead us closer to God.
—MSGR. EDWARD W. O'MALLEY

February 28

Light is sweet, and it is pleasant for the eyes to behold the sun.
—Ecclesiastes 11:7

SUNSETS are among the most beautiful memories of man. We can never have our fill of either seeing them or trying to describe them in paintings, in poems, and in music. And yet sunsets, in all their grandeur and mystery, are as nothing in the light of the breathtaking splendor of God.

IT SEEMS too good to be true, but God has destined us to see Him one day in all of His splendor. We poor little mortals, called to a life above and beyond our fondest hopes, our wildest dreams. It is a sad thing indeed then if we should let ourselves lose sight of this eternal goal and begin to wonder if all our struggles on earth are really worth the effort.

THE SAINTS never tire of telling us to hope in the Lord and to await His coming with joy and thankfulness, with songs and shouts of joy. Let us then rejoice!
—FATHER DONALD F. X. CONNOLLY

February 29

"Ask, and it will be given you; seek, and you will find; knock, and it will be opened to you. . . ." Matthew 7:7

MANY people find it hard to understand the words of our Lord: "Ask, and it will be given you; seek, and you will find; knock, and it will be opened to you. For every one who asks receives, and he who seeks finds, and to him who knocks it will be opened." They ask, but do not receive; they seek, but do not find; and their knocks go unanswered.

WE ARE a proud people and we think our ideas are super. We feel that life would be just one great thing after another if God would only grant us our requests. However, as we learn from the Old Testament, our ways are not God's ways and God's ways are not our ways. God knows far more than the knowledge of all men of all time — past, present and future. God knows that many of our requests would, if granted, be harmful to us, and His goodness will not allow that to happen.

THE Our Father's "Thy will be done," and our Blessed Mother's "Be it done to me according to thy word," must also be ours in our prayers of petition.

—MSGR. RALPH G. KUTZ

March 1

Take your share of suffering as a good soldier of Christ Jesus.
—2 Timothy 2:3

M ARCH is the month named after Mars, the pagan god of war. It's a good month for the soldiers of Christ to be taken up with their annual spring maneuvers, which we call the season of Lent.

A GOOD soldier keeps fit all year round. But he needs special periods of concentrated exercise so that he can renew his basic training, tone up his muscles, discover his weak spots, and work out new strategies against the latest weapons of the enemy.

IT MAY SEEM strange that the Prince of Peace came to bring a sword. But Christ's very message is that a man gains the right to peace of heart only by taking up the sword against the lazy, indifferent, unloving, self-satisfying pagan who is never far beneath the surface of the human heart. There is a pagan Mars in the calendar of every man's character. He's the false god who battles unceasingly against the Prince of Peace. Take sides this Lent.

—FATHER JOSEPH GALLAGHER

March 2

So faith, hope, love abide, these three; but the greatest of these is love. —I Corinthians 13:13

G OD comes to modern souls not through their reason which is weak, but through their hunger which is great. If we fail to understand the way their hearts work, we will drive them from God. Their mockery and their sneers are only masks, which in their hearts they want us to see through. They are to be less censured than those of us who hate them because they hate us.

MILLIONS are fluttering like wounded birds around the Rock. Get on your knees for them. Be the sign of the eternal on the face of the earth, the mystery of faith against the mystery of iniquity.

IF YOU GO into the world with the idea that everyone is an enemy or a bigot, you will be surprised how many enemies and bigots you will meet; but if you go into the world with the assurance that everyone is looking for Our Lord, you will be surprised how many lovable people you will meet. Plant love where you do not find it, and then everyone will be lovable.

—BISHOP FULTON J. SHEEN

March 3

The light of the eyes rejoices the heart, and good news refreshes the bones. —Proverbs 15:30

OLD MRS. CHU could not read, yet she spent hours in church with a prayer book. One day the missioner asked her how she used the book.

"AS YOU SEE," replied Mrs. Chu, "my book contains blank sheets of colored paper: red, white, yellow, purple, green, blue. I look at the red sheet, and I think of joy and happiness because red is the Chinese color for joy. I look at the white sheet, it is the color of purity. I think of myself, my children, my children's children. Yellow and purple and green are the sunset, a beautiful gateway at the end of the road.

"BLUE IS HEAVEN. When I get to blue, I look at Our Lord in the tabernacle, and He looks back at me. Time is so short when I use my prayer book!"

LIKE MRS. CHU, each one of us should daily meditate on the great truths God has revealed to us.

—FATHER ALBERT J. NEVINS, M.M.

March 4

All the days of the afflicted are evil, but a cheerful heart has a continual feast. —Proverbs 15:15

CRISIS, crisis, everything seems to come out as a crisis, Lord. There used to be so much talk of adolescent crisis, as if when one passed through that, the worst would be over. Yet as I look around me, as I go on in age, I realize that every stage has its own crisis.

MY SON, why do you always want things to stop, and stand still? You seem to want something to be over and done with. That is not the way with human life, my son.

BUT, LORD, no one said there would be crises all through life — these seem only like variations on the themes of adolescent crises. Is this new Lord, or just my life?

NO, MY SON, it is not new, not just your life. People seem hesitant to admit to crises, that is all. Could it be, my son, that twenty-one is really not the peak year of life?

—FATHER KEN J. BERNARD

March 5

. . . If a man is overtaken in any trespass, you who are spiritual should restore him in a spirit of gentleness. Look to yourself, lest you too be tempted. —Galatians 6:1

THIS is the season of penance and the Church in her instructions on Lent makes it very clear that the nature of this season has not changed. We have a choice in the matter of penance. There is no specific obligation laid down by the general law of the Church, but we do have an obligation to do penance.

THE PENANCE, however, should be aimed, not at making us simply uncomfortable, or taking on some hardship, although this is definitely part of the tough business of penance. Penance should be aimed at making us better persons and reforming our habits.

THE READINGS in today's Mass speak of having a "broken and humbled heart." They also indicate the kind of penance and the kind of fasting that are acceptable to God.

—FATHER BLASE SCHAUER, O.P.

March 6

You are no longer strangers and sojourners, but you are fellow citizens with the saints and members of the household of God. . . .
—Ephesians 2:19

"IF you really love one another properly, there must be sacrifice." — Mother Teresa

ONCE a group of professors and teachers came to Calcutta. When they were leaving they asked, "Tell us something we can do when we get home to improve our lives." Mother Teresa's reply was, "Smile at one another. Have the wife smile at the husband, and the husband smile at the wife and children, especially when you are tired, when you are in a bad mood, when you feel like breaking everything." Then one of the visitors asked her, "Mother, have you ever been married?" Her immediate answer was, "Yes, and sometimes I find it very difficult to smile at Jesus."

IN THIS anxious age of rushing and TV there is a deterioration of family life because we are all so busy. We have no time for our children or each other. Let us remember that our first responsibility is to our family. We must make our homes centers of compassion and love. Let's make time for our own and smile at one another.

—ALICE COLLINS

March 7

. . . Rejoice in so far as you share Christ's sufferings, that you may also rejoice and be glad when his glory is revealed. —I Peter 4:13

TWO African women, long ago, made up their minds to suffer any and all torments rather than to deny their faith in Jesus Christ. Their story is one of the great episodes of the days of persecution. They proved to the hilt that man's superior bravery is a pure myth.

WHEN THE HISTORY of modern persecution is written, how many times will their story be repeated? There is evidence seeping out beneath the Iron Curtain that our contemporary Perpetuas and Felicitys are the ones who are really baffling the enemies of God. Ordinary women, possessed of extraordinary grace and courage. Outstanding women, like Edith Stein, the German Carmelite, whose dreadful fate both shocks and thrills us.

"TODAY," said Felicity, "it is I who suffer; yet there is Another in me who suffers for me, because I suffer for Him."
—BISHOP ROBERT J. DWYER, Reno, Nevada

March 8

For the moment all discipline seems painful rather than pleasant; later it yields the peaceful fruit of righteousness. . . . —Hebrews 12:11

IN this sacred season of Lent we had better start, and without delay, to become practical about this business of the salvation of our immortal soul. We should mentally stand back from the world's occupations and preoccupations and ponder that we are here on this earth for only one essential purpose: to merit Heaven.

PERHAPS we have drifted too far away from the sound of God's words, so immersed are we in earthly affairs. Or it is even possible that we deliberately shielded our ears so that we could not hear Him, while we continued to enjoy illicitly the fruit of the forbidden tree. Lent is the time to drop all pretense, to search the soul, to see if there be anything wrong between our life and God's commandments. — (*Rock of Truth,* Rev. James J. McNally)
—FATHER JOSEPH E. MANTON, C.SS.R.

March 9

Let him turn away from evil and do right; let him seek peace and pursue it. —I Peter 3:11

L ENT is a period of basic training for the Christian who would be a reliable soldier in the army of his faith.

THE BASIC program of Lent is the intense practice of prayer and mortification so that the will might be strengthened and reason made dominant over the physical appetites. Like the military basic training, the Christian soldier's program of intense training in discipline of the spirit is intended to produce a man of dedication.

THE SOLDIER of Christ will prefer doing good rather than evil, and be dedicated to the things of God rather than enslaved to the things of man; this he will be because the days of Lent have their lesson. Prayer will have directed the intellect to its goal and set the will upon its object, both of which is God; mortification will have helped to put the body in its proper role of servant of reason.

—FATHER CHARLES W. PARIS

March 10

Thou didst clothe with skin and flesh, and knit me together with bones and sinews. —Job 10:11

I N his superb life of Christ (*To Know Christ*) Frank Sheed reminds us that the young Blessed Mother "never lost contact with God, God in her soul, God playing on the floor." This is a startling image for all its truth, but it pales before the feast of the Annunciation, and fact where God is in the Tabernacle as humbly as a piece of bread in a breadbox. The more you ponder, the more you marvel at the utter humility of Our Savior.

ON A CATHEDRAL altar with its gleaming marble, golden candlesticks, gorgeous flowers, jeweled monstrance, the simplest "Thing" there is the thin white Host. But how else could He remain among us, and be united to us, except by some such miracle as this? He lived and died but wanted to survive in our midst. So, vased in the slender monstrance is the fairest flower of all.

IF FROM the carpenter shop of Nazareth there had been preserved but one thing that Jesus had made, how we would treasure that relic! Today we rejoice that we have not here the relic but the Reality!

—FATHER JOSEPH E. MANTON, C.SS.R.

March 11

For everything there is a season, and a time for every matter under heaven. —Ecclesiastes 3:1

SPRING has not yet officially arrived, but it is in the air even though, in our part of the United States, that air is still crisp and the grass is not yet green. Only the pussy willows in our woods have sprouted, but they are a harbinger of greater things to come when the miracle of spring bursts forth again and the earth renews herself.

SPRING is a reminder that we too can and must renew. All of life is a dying and rising. Only by dying can we live again, live in Christ who as the Greek Liturgy expresses it, "is the day which is splendid with the light that knows no evening."

JESUS is Lord. He is alive. And because Christ is living, our hope too is alive. Though it might seem that confusion is very much in evidence in the world and consequently in the Church today, we know that the Holy Spirit is at work. Just as He once brought order out of the chaotic waters of creation, so He will bring order to the new creation won for us by Christ in His paschal mystery.

—SISTER ELIZABETH ANN CLIFFORD, O.L.V.M.

March 12

. . . He who utters slander is a fool. —Proverbs 10:18

FREEDOM of speech, freedom of assembly and other freedoms do offer the opportunity to men to make or break themselves — to make a good image of themselves, to improve their image, to cast serious doubts about their abilities, or to mark themselves off as hopeless cases. Oftentimes, one impetuous, untoward action can give a person an image that can be severely damaging.

ONE IS reminded of the valuable counsel given in the Book of Proverbs: "Even a fool, if he will hold his peace, shall be counted wise; and if he close his lips, a man of understanding." And the Book of Sirach provides this advice: "Weep for the dead, for his light has failed; and weep for the fool, for his understanding faileth. Weep but a little for the dead, for he is at rest. . . . The mourning for a fool and an ungodly man is all the days of their life."

ANCIENT, but ever new, too, is the proverb: "Fools rush in where angels dare to tread." A prudent man guards his every word.

—MSGR. RALPH G. KUTZ

March 13

"Blessed art thou, O Lord, God of our fathers, and worthy of praise."
—Daniel 3:1-3

IF God sometimes seems slow to answer our petitions, there are several possible reasons. One is that the delay is for the purpose of deepening our love and increasing our faith; the other is that God is urging us. God may defer for some time the granting of His gifts, that we might the more ardently pursue, not the gift but the Giver. Or we may be asking Him for something He wants us to learn we do not need.

A HIGHER form of prayer than petition — and a potent remedy against the externalization of life — is meditation. Meditation is a little like a daydream or a reverie, but with two important differences: in meditation we do not think about the world or ourselves, but about God. And instead of using the imagination to build idle castles in Spain, we use the will to make resolutions that will draw us nearer to one of the Father's mansions. Meditation is a more advanced spiritual act than "saying prayers."
—BISHOP FULTON J. SHEEN

March 14

There is another who is slow and needs help, who lacks strength and abounds in poverty; but the eyes of the Lord look upon him for his good.
—Sirach 11:12

HAVE you ever considered the hope that must be in the lives of the mentally ill, or the mentally retarded, of the handicapped or the poverty-stricken?

WHAT MUST their days be like, if they do not have hope? A constant existence of despair, of semi-life, never really seeing the sun through the clouds that shroud their every day. Without hope they live an existence that most of us never dream of.

BUT WHEN they have hope, when they are able to find strength in God, when, perhaps, someone gives them a helping hand that opens a new life — how beautiful is the return from near death! A life takes on a completely different meaning when it is filled with hope, or even given a small glimmer of it.

WHEN WE see such men, basing their entire souls on hope in God and man, how can we, more fortunate, not hope?
—MR. JAMES M. NUSBAUM, S.J.

March 15

"Father, if thou art willing, remove this cup from me; nevertheless not my will, but thine, be done." —Luke 22:42

"I AM not seeking my own will but the will of him who sent me" (John 5:30). This was the thrust of Christ's whole life and mission, to carry out the will of the Father. He told the Apostles on one occasion: "Doing the will of him who sent me . . . is my food" (John 4:34). In the Garden of Gethsemani, He prayed: "Not my will but thine be done" (Luke 22:42). When it had been done, He said on the cross: "Now it is finished" (John 19:30).

IN THE Our Father, we pray: "Thy will be done." This is the mainline commitment of our lives. Related to it is the search we have to make to find out what the will of God is for us. He makes it known clearly through Scripture, tradition and the experience of the Church in its teaching and sacramental life. He also makes it known in more mysterious ways in what have been called the "signs of the times" and the needs of people.

WITH THE AID of the Holy Spirit, we can learn to read these signs and how to respond to often neglected opportunities.
—FATHER FELICIAN A. FOY, O.F.M.

March 16

The Lord God formed man of dust from the ground, and breathed into his nostrils the breath of life. . . . —Genesis 2:7

BREATH has a powerful meaning for us. If we do not breathe we cannot live. If we do not share in the breath of God, if it does not fill all that we are, then we cannot live the way we are destined to.

BREATHING the breath of the Lord and allowing His strong yet gentle wind to come over our lives, makes us true instruments of His life. Where people are oppressed or treated unjustly, we speak the Word of God and criticize the injustice. Where people are lonely and neglected, we come in consolation and sacrifice for our brothers.

WHERE PEOPLE are celebrating their joys and loves, we join in their happiness. Wherever people are suffering and being helped and wherever people are coming together in loving community, that is where the Spirit of God is alive — that is where the name of God is being kept holy.
—JAMES M. SULLIVAN, M.M.

March 17

In return for my love they accuse me, even as I make prayer for them. —Psalms 109:4

MOST of us are liable to think of the saint as in heaven, glorified; not as he was on earth, mortified. We recall his triumph, not his ceaseless struggle against the same nature we ourselves drag along the road to salvation. It might be well then to listen to what Saint Patrick says of his heroic efforts:

"CONSTANTLY I used to pray in the daytime. Love of God and His fear increased more and more, and my faith grew and my spirit was stirred up, so that in a single day I said as many as a hundred prayers and at night nearly as many, so that I used to stay even in the woods and on the mountain (to this end).

"AND BEFORE the dawn I used to be aroused to prayer, in snow and frost and rain, nor was there any tepidity in me such as now I feel, because then the spirit was fervent within."

—FATHER G. JOSEPH GUSTAFSON, S.S.

March 18

He who loves his brother abides in the light . . . but he who hates his brother is in the darkness and walks in the darkness. . . .
—1 John 2:10-11

SOMEONE, besides God, has to start love somewhere. And this is what a Christian is called to do. And, interestingly, when we accept the rejection of others, with solid Christian motivation, in time they begin to accept us.

SINCE THE REJECTION, on their part, is basically on the unconscious level, they might not recognize their unconscious replacement of our acceptance of them for their rejection of us. All they know is that they are beginning to accept us. And it is enough.

IF WE BEGIN to love God because at first we love God's love for us, which, though somewhat selfish, is still acceptable to God, perhaps a starting point is loving God's love in our neighbor. Christ died for him, too.

—FATHER ROBERT THORSEN

March 19

. . . Joseph, being a just man. . . . —Matthew 1:19

T HERE is an invocation in the Litany of St. Joseph which sums up the life of the foster-father of Our Lord: "St. Joseph, most prudent." There is no action of St. Joseph which was not marked by prudence.

PRUDENCE is another term for common sense. Whether it was in complete compliance with the biddings of the angel or in the maintenance of golden silence or in his care for the Child Jesus and the Blessed Mother, St. Joseph gives the perfect example of being always calm, ever collected, possessed of the common sense of complete submissiveness to God's holy will at all times and in all circumstances.

LIKE MARTHA whom Our Lord described as being troubled about many things, we let ourselves get all het up about all kinds of things and we forget the one thing that is necessary. We need to be like St. Joseph whose common sense led him to do things God's way.

—MSGR. RALPH G. KUTZ

March 20

Jesus sat down and called the twelve; and he said to them, "If any one would be first, he must be last of all and servant of all."
—Mark 30:35

F ROM the Gospels we read: "He that is greatest among you shall be your servant. He that exalteth himself shall be humbled and he that humbleth himself shall be exalted" (Matthew 23:11, 12).

POPE JOHN XXIII used as his title, "Servant of the servants of God." Our Lord both by word and example condemned pride and praised humility. His own social position and that of His Mother and St. Joseph, the family of a poor, village carpenter, speak more eloquently than words. The outstanding virtue of Our Blessed Mother and of St. Joseph was their humility.

WE SHOULD learn from those who are closest to our Blessed Savior. "What majesty surrounds the silent and hidden figure of St. Joseph on account of the spirit with which he accomplished the mission entrusted to him by God? For true worth of a man is not measured by the tinsel of resounding results, but by the inner attitudes of order and good will." —*(Pope John XXIII)*
—BISHOP LEO R. SMITH, Buffalo, New York

March 21

"Blessed are the pure in heart, for they shall see God."
—Matthew 5:8

T HE Gospels contain the pattern of Christian prayer. It is based upon faith in God as Father and Friend, and the open acknowledgment of our dependence upon Him. At the same time, it recognizes that a change must take place in ourself, if prayer is to have any meaning at all. We work for the coming of *His* Kingdom; we forgive those who injure us; we stay away from those things that take us away from God.

THERE IS a phrase in the Our Father that is not always clear in the English translation, even though it is in Latin and Greek: *Thy will be done on earth as it is in Heaven.*

IN THE Latin and Greek it says: As Your Will is done in Heaven, so may it be done on earth, with the meaning that the heavenly situation is the model of the earthly one. In Heaven, God's sovereignty is total and complete, all wills are attuned to His, all hearts are united in His will, and in His love. It is this model that we aim for: positively, continually, personally.

—FATHER CLIFFORD STEVENS

March 22

He is the source of your life in Christ Jesus, whom God made our wisdom, our righteousness and sanctification and redemption. . . .
—I Corinthians 1:30

W HEN we look into the personality of Jesus, we discover a man of great charm, majesty, dignity, gentleness, compassion, and love. It is an overwhelmingly impressive personality. It is no wonder Philip exclaimed to his friends after his first meeting with Jesus: "We have found him of whom Moses did write!"

JESUS was a man without sin. He could challenge His enemies: "Which of you can convict me of sin?" His whole work of Redemption was in opposition to sin. He delivered the human race from sin. He gave to His apostles and their successors the power to forgive sin.

IT IS ONE of the tragic ironies of history that the God Man who so hated sin should die because of sin. Every sin committed has a share in putting Jesus on the cross. Can any sin be worth the terrible price of killing Christ?

—FATHER ALBERT J. NEVINS, M.M.

March 23

"Abba, Father, all things are possible to thee . . . yet not what I will, but what thou wilt." —Mark 14:36

" "TAKE this chalice from Me." Who can fathom the depths of the agony in this prayer of Our Lord in the garden? Many theology books could not make more clear the reality of Jesus' human experience as He faced the horrors of His death, rejected, betrayed, deserted, misunderstood and — even in the presence of His disciples — alone.

THE AGONY of this moment is the measure of His love for mankind and of His identification with the human plight. He had taken on himself the burden of the human race.

HE HAD accepted the guilt of all that all men had done, of all the sins of mankind, my sins among them. It was as if He were responsible for — almost as if He had committed all the sins of mankind. God was laying on Him the iniquities of us all.

—FATHER THOMAS M. BREW, S.J.

March 24

He began to invoke a curse on himself and to swear, "I do not know this man of whom you speak." And immediately the cock crowed a second time. . . . —Mark 14:71-72

THE stark simplicity and directness of St. Mark's Passion, read at Mass, stamp the Cross indelibly on our memory. We remember it as St. Peter did, for tradition tells us that the first Pope dictated this Gospel to his disciple Mark. That is why Our Lord's prediction, "Before the cock crows twice, thou wilt deny me thrice," takes such prominence. Peter could never forget his cowardice.

NEITHER COULD he forget the divine forgiveness. Coward though he had been, he was still the Keeper of the Keys, still the Shepherd of the Flock, still the Rock on which Christ would build His Church.

THE STORY of Peter's frailty and Christ's understanding mercy is the great charter of hope for all of us. How many times have we imitated Peter in his weakness, only to be lifted up and set on our feet again by the Lord of boundless pardon. The real question, however, is whether our repentance matches Peter's. Other peoples' tears are no substitute for our own.

—BISHOP ROBERT J. DWYER, Reno, Nevada

March 25

Blessed are you among women, and blessed is the fruit of your womb! —Luke 1:42

THE Annunciation of the Lord deserves the thundering dignity of its long name, because it differed so much from all other mere "announcements." There have been announcements of the birth of princes, and of the assassinations of kings; announcements of new presidents and new popes; announcements of wars declared and peace treaties signed — thousands of announcements.

BUT IN the headlines of history there never had been an announcement like this: "God Comes On Earth!" For, the Feast of the Annunciation celebrates the day when the Archangel Gabriel announced to the Virgin Mary that she was to become the Mother of God. And when she consented, the Word was made Flesh — to be born nine months later on the twenty-fifth of December.

BUT IT all began today. Everything that went before, patriarchs and prophets, were preparation. Everything afterward, a natural effect. This was *the event.*

—FATHER JOSEPH E. MANTON, C.SS.R.

March 26

Sing praises to the Lord, for he has done gloriously . . . Shout and sing for joy. . . . —Isaiah 12:5-6

"WE must proclaim Christ, by the way we talk, by the way we walk, the way we laugh, by our life, so everyone will know, we belong to Him." — *(Mother Teresa)*

RECENTLY while visiting the Sisters in Guatemala, Mother Teresa announced that in Holland they had named a turnip for her. Puzzled, the Sisters questioned, "A turnip, Mother?" "Yes, you know, that flower!" It was, of course, a tulip. They all had a good laugh. Mother Teresa's sense of humor is delightful. To spend time in her presence is refreshing, because of her simplicity, her calm presence, her humility and unpretentiousness, all of which put one at ease.

WHEN with Mother Teresa, one senses her lack of critical, self-righteous judgment. On the contrary, one is accepted "as is" with a bright smile. And wouldn't it be a wonderful world if we all could be the same?

—ALICE COLLINS

March 27

"Let not your hearts be troubled; believe in God, believe also in me. In my Father's house are many rooms; if it were not so, would I have told you that I go to prepare a place for you?" —John 14:1-2

I think I see, Lord, that there is room in our world for all kinds of people. Your lifegiving action has made us realize that there is room for the weak, the sick, the alcoholic, the mentally unstable, in our own existence.

YES, MY SON, but more than that. It is not just that you grant them room to exist, that you tolerate them around. You must grant them room to share. Let the weak share in your strength, and the mentally unstable share in your sobriety and the anti-social character can share in your trust. Help fill in what is lacking, my son.

I WILL TRY, Lord, but You ask the difficult.

YES, MY SON, for it is difficult to build the new earth.
—FATHER KEN J. BERNARD

March 28

In him we live and move and have our being. . . . —Acts 17:28

YOUTH finds its proper field for doing battle for Christ in the home, the classroom, and their related activities.

PRAYER HELPS a modern young person to sift the silt of a pleasure loving, ease seeking, less-than-honest code of conduct from the clear course of spiritual happiness and honest accomplishment, which alone can make life gratifying.

MORTIFICATION ENABLES the young to be obedient and respectful to parents and to all authority, to accept and profit from the discipline of true study, to reject the social code whose morality is "everything goes — just don't get caught."

LOVE For Christ generates that deep and abiding loyalty of which only the boundlessness of youthful idealism seems capable. As Christ is better known, and known as personal Leader, the dedication and attachment to Him and His standard becomes the foundation and crown of life's activities.
—FATHER CHARLES W. PARIS

March 29

O our God hearken to the prayer of thy servant and to his supplications. —Daniel 9:17

PRAYER — intensified and purified — has hopefully been one of our special Lenten practices this year. Today's Mass reminds us of that with its opening words, "O God, hear my prayer."

WE WILL NEVER understand the true meaning of prayer until we see it as an essential means for getting us to do God's Will, rather than the other way around. In pagan religions the purpose of magic was to give human beings power and control over the supernatural. In Christianity, the role of prayer is to give the Divine Will more penetrating impact on our ideas, decisions and deeds.

WE ARE NOT forbidden to voice to God our needs as we see them. Such prayers remind us of the real source of all blessing, and make us scrutinize our wishes in the searching light of faith. But the great prayer still remains, "Not mine, but Thy Will be done."

—FATHER JOSEPH GALLAGHER

March 30

The Lord is in his holy temple. . . . —Psalms 11:4

THE artist locks himself up in his studio to do his work; the scientist in his laboratory. Each occupation needs its proper atmosphere and its suitable place. Theaters are not set aside for dancing and restaurants are not used for football games. Lent should find me often in the House of God.

DAVID longed for the House of the Lord, for the temple worship that brought him into God's Presence, and the prophet longed for the courts of the Lord. Many of our happiest and loveliest moments are the moments spent in a holy atmosphere. That is why it is customary to go to monasteries for retreats; the very walls speak of God and the silence and solitude encourage thought and meditation.

CHURCHES, to accomplish their purpose must be used. We must, in a sense, lock ourselves up in them and do that work for God which is the very nourishment of our souls. In this restless, hurrying age, we must slow down, at least during Lent, take a breathing spell, get our bearings. The parish church is there for that purpose. "I love your tabernacles, O Lord of Hosts."

—FATHER BLASE SCHAUER, O.P.

March 31

You must also be ready; for the Son of man is coming at an hour you do not expect. —Matthew 24:44

SECONDS, minutes, hours, days, weeks, months and years are but measuring sticks of time; yet, they are important factors in the life of every individual. Even the so-called split-second frequently makes a great difference in the life and affairs of men. As men look over their own past, they inevitably wish that — either for the sake of further enjoyment or for warding off disappointment — they might be able to re-live many moments. But, the past is beyond recall; the memories of its experiences, whether good or bad, can but act to guide one's future actions.

IT IS NOT given to us to know what the future holds in store for us. Everyone wants continued prosperity; everyone wants life and health, but accidents and illness will take their heavy toll. Many will be the wants, many the enjoyments, many the satisfactions; but, many too will be the sorrows.

THE BEST formula for living the future was given to us by our Blessed Savior: "Do not lay up for yourselves treasures on earth . . . but lay up for yourselves treasures in Heaven."

—MSGR. RALPH G. KUTZ

April 1

. . . Folly is the garland of fools. —Proverbs 14:24

A PRIL Fool's Day is an observance founded on healthy wit that leaves no sore but rather a fond remembrance. Pleasing wit is invigorating. It drives away gloom. It is a contagion not to be feared.

TO FOOL another, friend or stranger, on April 1st in a charitable way, makes friends for a lifetime. It is generally a day of surprising wit, found where least expected — as in an unsmiling individual who is sometimes wrongfully judged and considered rather backward or slow.

ONE SUCH person kept 180 million people laughing for years by writing two lines in the daily newspapers. Asked for his secret he said, "I never met a person I did not like."

ALL FOLLOWERS of Christ are under command to love one another as He loved us. With God's special grace, that can be had for the asking, one can like any person if he realizes that that person is made to the image of God himself.

—FATHER TOM MARTIN, S.J.

April 2

Be doers of the word, and not hearers only, deceiving your-selves. —James 1:22

T HE secret of living successfully and happily is being able to do the most with the moment we have at hand.

THE FUTURE it is true must not be left to chance. But if we are always dreaming of the great and wonderful things of tomorrow we will never have time to get anything done today.

TRUTH IS the same in the spiritual life as it is in material things. All dreams must be followed by actual work. We may dream about how advanced we may be in the spiritual life by the end of the year or ten years hence but unless we get this or that fault out of our life today we are not going to advance one whit. The spiritual life is practical even if not material. Big success does not come all at once like a winning ticket on the sweepstakes because the spiritual life is not a gamble. But each little positive action grows and in time accumulates. Let's not despise or neglect the little things. If we do, we will never get any farther than we are. We will be great *dreamers* but little *doers.*

—FATHER JAMES D. MORIARTY

April 3

. . Grace to you and peace from God our Father and the Lord Jesus Christ. —Romans 1:7

IT is well to start each day by making the Morning Offering. As soon as you arise, bless yourself and say: "O Jesus, through the Immaculate Heart of Mary, I offer Thee my prayers, works and sufferings of this day for all the intentions of Thy Sacred Heart, in union with the Holy Sacrifice of the Mass throughout the world, in reparation for my sins, for the intentions of all our Associates and in particular for the intention of the Apostleship of Prayer."

BY SAYING this prayer devoutly, you consecrate every thought, word and deed to almighty God, thus making them meritorious for you.

THIS IS THE MEANING of the famous saying of St. Paul: "Whether you eat or drink, or whatsoever else you do, do all to the glory of God." Your Morning Offering turns all your thoughts, words and deeds into prayers. Throughout the day recall your Morning Offering and renew your intentions.

—FATHER JOHN A. O'BRIEN

April 4

As obedient children, do not be conformed to the passions of your former ignorance, but as he who called you is holy, be holy yourselves in your conduct. —I Peter 1:14-15

MY problem is not the mistakes I make but honestly and sincerely admitting them. I blame others easily. I even include God in my accusations. I try to live a good life. I don't want to be a self-satisfied Pharisee up in front reminding God of all I do for Him. Deep in my hidden, safe-from-embarrassment thought, I'm rather pleased with my life's record. Then why am I punished?

PILATE judged three men guilty of death. On the cross one rebelled and cried to be taken down. One admitted "he received the just reward for his sins." One silently offered His innocent Blood that He might "take away the sin of the world."

HUMILITY and justice in suffering the cross merited a Redeemer and His redeemed companion a "today in Paradise." Unwillingness to admit guilt and justly accept its punishment made a criminal impenitent and rebellious — he wasted his Calvary.

—V. REV. BERNARDINE SHINE, O.S.B.

April 5

Whatever is born of God overcomes the world; and this is the victory that overcomes the world, our faith. —I John 5:4

A RCHBISHOP Fulton Sheen once said: "What is important in life is not what happens, but how we react to what happens." This thought was previously stated in a little different way by the valiant Mrs. Rose Kennedy who has suffered so many tragedies. She said: "I'm not going to be vanquished by these events."

THE TRUE Christian says with the Blessed Mother: "Be it done unto me according to Thy word." Or as Jesus prayed the night before His death: "Not my will but Thine be done." His prayer in agony was but an echo of the beautiful prayer He gave us, the Our Father, which says: "Thy will be done on earth as it is in heaven."

BY ACCEPTING God's will — we show Him our love. We are not brave enough or bold enough as the great saints to go out and do heroic deeds for God, but all of us can accept with humble resignation the things that come into our lives which we cannot change. And this shows fortitude and love.

—FATHER RAWLEY MYERS

April 6

Bless the Lord, all things that grow on the earth, sing praise to him and highly exalt him for ever. —Daniel 3:54

A MONG all the scents of Spring, none is more impressive than the soil with its growing warmth. If you get on your knees for some gardening you know the smell and the meaning of the soil. Turn it over between your fingers, gently. Know it better. The firm permanence of it. The molding and flocculenting processes that build it. The rocks and plants. The sun and the rain that went into it long before a plow or hoe ever scarred it. It is there. It will remain many Springs after you are gone.

PLOWING, the man on the land senses this. Once in a while he stops and looks. Then, kneels to feel it. You feel the mystery as you kneel. Yet, you cannot fathom it. A bud. A leaf. A bloom. These, deeper than understanding itself.

THESE COME from the molds of the past: generations and centuries far removed, from a past and a soil you feel between your fingers as you kneel and instinctively ponder the miracle of God.

—MARIE LAYNE

April 7

You are a chosen race, a royal priesthood, a holy nation, God's own people, that you may declare the wonderful deeds of him who called you out of darkness into his marvelous light. —I Peter 2:9

THE Easter-time is agleam with light. It is the light from the empty tomb. Christ, rising from the dead, has scattered the darkness of death, has rent the curtain between time with its mortality, and eternity, with its immortality, and the splendor of the everlasting shines into the world.

ST. PETER tells us, in a passage used by the Church in Easter's Mass, that God has called us out of darkness into His marvelous light and that it is our duty to proclaim His exploits (First Epistle II, 9). As Christians, we share the light of the victorious Christ. The light of truth is in us. We have to spread it to others.

SO MANY know nothing of it. They frolic or plod through life, are at last borne down by its difficulties, and go to the grave as to their final end. And some of them are our friends, neighbors, associates at work. From us they have got not one least glimmer of the light of Christ. This is a failure which should trouble us and prompt us to be effective bearers of the light.

—MSGR. JOHN S. KENNEDY

April 8

Jesus said . . . "Have you believed because you have seen me? Blessed are those who have not seen and yet believe." —John 20:29

WHEN Christ showed himself to the Apostles they were overjoyed, and their hearts filled with thoughts of love for Him, and they witnessed to Him through the whole world. If we are to be witnesses to Jesus our hearts must be filled with Him as were those of the Apostles. We have to see Him too.

WE SEE the Master in the Gospels and the other parts of the New Testament. If we read these regularly, the Lord will be always before our eyes and we can't help loving Him. It is only when we fail to keep Him before our eyes that He becomes hazy and distant.

OFTEN when we attend Mass, it is only a religious exercise — even dull. This is because we haven't collected our thoughts. For the first part of Mass we should be saying "This is it; I am going to touch Christ — He is really coming to me."

—MSGR. MAURICE COONEY

April 9

Sing to the Lord with thanksgiving; make melody to our God upon the lyre! —Psalms 147:7

TO lead a good life does not demand all work and no play, run and no rest, duty without diversion. True, as sinners we should fast and abstain, repent and retreat, sacrifice and suffer for the suffering we've caused Christ, who loves us. But because He does love us, He designed good times. Use them in appreciation and in all the countless forms they take!

THE STORY of that great 14th century saint, Teresa of Avila, is one to remember. A visitor was scandalized when seeing this holy woman happily eating partridge. Wisely she told him, "There is a time for partridge and a time for penance."

GOD NEVER intended that we travel through life on our knees and with long faces. He invented enjoyment for us not only to embrace, but to share it with others . . . finding Him in others through happy, healthy recreation. Remember, Christ himself began His public life in the sociability of a wedding reception.

—JO CURTIS DUGAN

April 10

. . . In the name of the Father and of the Son and of the Holy Spirit. —Matthew 28:19

IN the sacramental life of the Church, we have always with us the Cross. Our children are baptized with the Sign of the Cross; and with holy chrism they are confirmed with the same sign. In his confessional the priest raises his hand in absolution over the penitent sinner and pardon is given with the Sign of the Cross.

IN THE LAST agony of the dying, when the priest comes with the holy oils to bring final comfort and consolation, the anointing of all the senses — the eyes, ears, nose, lips, the hands and the feet — each and every one is touched with the Sign of the Cross.

YOU CAN see how persistent is the Church in her teaching. Her children, however slow in mind and heart to learn her dearest lesson, have always somewhere about them, on their person or in their homes, the image of Our Blessed Lord upon His Cross.

—FATHER ALBERT A. MURRAY, C.S.P.

April 11

Let your heart cheer you in the days of your youth. . . .
—Ecclesiastes 11:9

A CHILD'S concept of love is limited, in that he perceives generally only the "good" side of this noblest of emotions. He does not, if he's fortunate, experience the pain which so often accompanies true love. He knows the secure joy of being offered ice cream, of being hugged before bedtime; this is his world, safe and uncomplicated.

HOW DIFFERENT is a child's innocent idea of love from our more realistic and experienced one. And so we glance tolerantly and reminiscently upon the "puppy love" of the young, all the while keeping the knowledge to ourselves that love hurts, as well as glorifies.

THERE WILL be time enough for a child to comprehend that to love is to surrender, to meet oneself and then to leave oneself. All too soon, a child will gain knowledge with maturity, and thus come to realize that to love is to crucify oneself for another. And aware of this, he will better understand the reason for the Greatest Love. "Love one another as I have loved you."

—BARBARA J. SIEMINSKI

April 12

His delight is in the law of the Lord, and on his law he meditates day and night. —Psalms 1:3

C HEERFULLY, an eighty-eight-year-old man looked back on his life. He pondered the reply when asked the secret of his happy outlook on life. Smiling, he said each morning, without fail, he recited to himself words his mother taught him when he was very young: "Something happy is on the way, 'cause God sends His love to me today."

EACH DAY, he awakens with this thought spinning in his brain and finds some measure of joy and blessing before the day ends.

REJOICE in blessings you know. There is joy in living. The beauty of creation. Hundreds of things happening each day bring joy. Thank God for all. When the day ends, you will feel filled with an exhilarating joy realizing how much good your day has brought you. Be trustworthy of God.

—MARIE LAYNE

April 13

". . . My groans are many and my heart is faint."
—Lamentations 1:22

THE root of modern evils is not ignorance of man's eternal destiny and the means to attain it. Rather it is lethargy of the spirit, weakness of the will, and coldness of the heart. Men so stricken by this disease try to excuse themselves by seeking shelter in the darkness of the past, and seek an alibi in errors, old and new. We must work upon their wills.

FACE UP to the present condition of your city and ours. Make sure that needs are well defined, that available forces are well rearmed. Invite all men of good will. Let their law be unconditional fealty to Jesus Christ and His teachings.

NOW IS THE TIME, beloved children! Now is the time to be firm and decisive and to shake off this fatal lethargy! It is the time for all good men, for all who are anxious for the world's destiny, to come together and close their ranks. It is time we rise from sleep, for our salvation is nigh! — *(Pope Pius XII)*
—FATHER G. JOSEPH GUSTAFSON, S.S.

April 14

. . . Let your laughter be turned to mourning and your joy to dejection. Humble yourselves before the Lord and he will exalt you.
—James 4:9-10

MANY years ago the Irish-American playwright, Eugene O'Neill, wrote a poetic drama which he called "Lazarus Laughed." Its theme was that the Lazarus of the Gospel, the story of whose summoning back from death, was made so completely and unutterably happy by the brief glimpse could not possibly explain what he had seen, only laugh at the foolishness of men who could or would not seek first the Kingdom of God.

NOW O'NEILL doubtless made use of a good deal of poetic license in writing his play. But his basic idea is pretty near the truth, that from the point of view of God and eternity most of our petty anxieties in this life are only worth laughing at.

SANCTITY no less than sanity very largely depends on our being wise enough to laugh at ourselves. Yet how solemnly we take ourselves, and how much we resent being made to look foolish.
—BISHOP ROBERT J. DWYER, Reno, Nevada

April 15

I will sing to my God a new song. . . . —Judith 16:13

SEEING prayer as friendship makes it easier to survive some of its difficult moments. No one prays for long without finding that it can be a dull and apparently unrewarding experience. It can seem like a waste of time, or a form of self-alienation. Like friendship, however, it can't be measured by its practical utility.

FRIENDSHIPS are based on love, not utility. Because the friendship in this case is between God and man, it is inevitable that it reach a point where man feels that he is walking in unknown territory. Mystics, like St. John of the Cross, find this quite normal. "On this road (of prayer), to enter the road means to leave it."

THE CLOSER man comes to God, the greater the feeling of obscurity and emptiness becomes. However, he keeps on walking because he knows his friend is there.

—FATHER ROMAN GINN, O.C.S.O.

April 16

And as they were eating, he took bread, and blessed, and broke it, and gave it to them, and said, "Take; this is my body." And he took a cup, and when he had given thanks he gave it to them, and they all drank of it. And he said to them, "This is my blood of the covenant, which is poured out for many." —Mark 14:22-24

THE institution of the Holy Eucharist, the First Mass and the First Ordination are celebrated on Holy Thursday. Within the framework of the Passion and Death of Christ, these great actions are overshadowed. The Apostles themselves probably did not grasp the significance of these events until after the Resurrection.

SO the Church wisely postpones the solemnity of these actions until the Feast of Corpus Christi. Instead, the liturgy puts emphasis on the prophetic fulfillment of Christ's saving action. He is the Christ, the anointed of the Father. Chrism is blessed by the bishop for the whole diocese, to emphasize the unity of the Church and its members in Christ. The chrism will be used to anoint new Christians.

THE Gospel tells the significant story of Christ washing the feet of the Apostles. The law of love includes service of one's neighbor. Christ made this abundantly clear.

—FATHER CHARLES DOLLEN

April 17

Pray at all times in the Spirit, with all prayer and supplication. To that end keep alert with all perseverance. . . . —Ephesians 6:18

PERSEVERANCE in prayer is a promise of endurance to the end. Whosoever does not pray is lost.

PRAYER is an exertion, it needs an effort; without at least that effort there is little hope for the future. Pray sincerely and humbly, however halting and imperfect your prayer may seem to be owing to human frailty and many distractions.

IF YOU GIVE up prayer, even for a short time, you risk Heaven. You lag behind and you may never make up your loss. The truest prayer for a Catholic is bound up with the reception of the Sacraments. Neglect those and you begin to stumble and fall.

IF YOU are faithful in receiving the Sacraments, everything is in your favor, and you can reasonably count on the Grace of God to bring life's journey to a happy end. Especially is this true of the Eucharist. To postpone your Communions is to suffer a setback in your spiritual progress. A starved soul cannot run swiftly in the paths of faith.

—FATHER ALBERT A. MURRAY, C.S.P.

April 18

Your wife will be like a fruitful vine within your house; your children will be like olive shoots around your table . . . Thus shall the man be blessed who fears the Lord. —Psalms 128:3-4

THE funny thing about happiness is that you can't keep it unless you give it away. A husband cannot be happy unless his wife is happy too. Mothers cannot be happy unless they make their little ones happy too.

THE SAME is true of health. If we in America do not export our medicines and medical knowledge we will be insecure. You can't have a healthy little enclave in the midst of a diseased world. The great influenza epidemics show us that. We must also export prosperity to other lands or our economy breaks down because we have no customers.

WE CAN'T climb alone; we have to help the others or we perish ourselves. Christ saw it first and taught us, "It is in giving that we receive."

—MSGR. MAURICE COONEY

April 19

I therefore, a prisoner for the Lord, beg you to lead a life worthy of the calling to which you have been called . . . Grace was given to each of us according to the measure of Christ's gift. —Ephesians 4:1, 7

A DOCTOR who had practiced medicine for five years asked his pastor, "Do you think I have a vocation to the priesthood?" "I do not know, you have not given it a chance. Ask the bishop." The doctor did ask the bishop and received the same answer.

HE CLOSED his clinic, sold everything, presented himself at the seminary. The rector fitted him in a new cassock. The putting on of the cassock decided everything. He was at peace, felt he made no mistake.

HE WAS ORDAINED. He is now a Monsignor, has erected a large church, grade and high school and has guided hundreds of converts.

WHEN the Holy Spirit gently speaks, give Him a chance, burn the bridges as Caesar did when crossing the Rubicon. Worldly possessions and successes will attract, but grace will triumph.
—FATHER TOM MARTIN, S.J.

April 20

"Do not be afraid, Mary, for you have found favor with God."
—Luke 1:30

HOW lovely is our Lady! Her large and beautiful eyes could tell a thousand tales. Her hands could sketch the deepest love of all the earth. Her heart could enclose the whole of creation. Her "yes" has filled the silent void of eternal peace.

BLESSED is she because she believed, because she heard the Father call her name and she never doubted that she could respond. Blessed is she because she has been a mother — and blessed are all mothers in her. Blessed is Mary, the virgin, because she touched the pulse of never-ending love. She did not have to say "yes." She did not have to heed the call of her Father, except insofar as she was prepared to be holy. She didn't have to endure such sorrow as she did but for her love of God and His love for her. But she did say "yes." She did heed His call and she did suffer sorrow.

OH, LOVELY MOTHER, we look to you as a model of womanhood and holiness. You are the honor and the glory of your people.
—T. TIMOTHY DELANEY

April 21

. . . Since we are justified by faith, we have peace with God through our Lord Jesus Christ. —Romans 5:1

BEING too close can make us miss the meaning of an event. A person watching TV often sees a close, fast play better than a fan at the World Series. The TV observer borrows the camera's quick eye to see the game.

FAITH is like the camera's eye. It gets a better close-up view of God's world. The Faith that believes though it does not see, always has a more exact view. Seeing says: "As it looks to me." Faith says: "It is."

LIGHT FAILS sometimes and misleads. The light of Faith never fails. It grows to the blinding vision of heaven. The light of Faith never deceives. I'm not to be pitied because I do not see but believe. "Blessed are they who have not seen but have believed."

—V. REV. BERNARDINE SHINE, O.S.B.

April 22

"Son, you are always with me, and all that is mine is yours."
—Luke 15:31

THE story of the Prodigal Son is well known but often forgotten. How often we behave as that son behaved? According to the story the prodigal son left his home and went away to a distant land where he wasted his fortune and finally ended up feeding swine. This has often been our manner of action.

WHEN WE leave the Church, forget what she tells us about Christ, go ahead and do what we feel like doing without any questions asked, we waste a fortune of love. By baptism we have become God's children in a special way, yet by our sins we behave as if we never knew God at all.

YET GOD is good. As the father received his son and put on him new clothes and a ring, and killed the fattened calf and made a feast for him, so does God, and more than that. This parable, coupled with that of the lost sheep, are but faint images of what happens when a sinner returns to God.

—MR. VICTOR DEGABRIELE, S.J.

April 23

Let the earth bless the Lord; let it sing praise to him and highly exalt him for ever. —Daniel 3:52

L ORD renew in me the promise of springtime. Help me to be aware of the parables You speak to me, through the earth and the sky You have created. When I see the young green of budding trees and tender grass, help me to praise You. Help me to rejoice in the springing of new life out of the death of winter.

WHEN I CATCH sight of the flicker of birds on the wing and hear their clear piercing spring song, let my heart lift with them. Let my heart soar and sing for love of Thee. When I buy seeds and plant them let me tremble in awe at the power encased in these small hard fragments. Let me realize that I too hold precious seeds of growth and fruitfulness within me.

LORD LET ME TRUST that You will open the fragments of divine life locked tight inside me. You alone can make them come alive, grow and bear fruit.

—BETTY WICKHAM

April 24

See what love the Father has given us, that we should be called children of God; and so we are. —I John 3:1

I MBUED with the great deeds of saints, who have died for Christ, we may often wonder how it is possible for us to become one in these modern days. Life, today, is not different than before. Each century has produced its own peculiar brand of problems. Each century, yet to come, will continue to have them. If the saints, in their glory now, had a simple time of living, we can be sure they would not be in God's realm today. Sainthood implies the conquering of difficulties, adversities, and temptations. Sainthood implies battling severely with every form of known worldly vice and corruption.

EACH OF US can travel the road to sainthood in his own way. For each, there will be snarls to unravel, devils to combat. It is up to us how we will travel that road. For each of us there is a special brand of sainthood.

WE CANNOT wish our temporal lives to be a bed of roses and hope for an eternal life the same as theirs. Our bed of roses, in the eternal, will be ours if we persevere.

—MARIE LAYNE

April 25

And they went forth and preached everywhere, while the Lord worked with them and confirmed the message by the signs that attended it. —Mark 16:19

TODAY, the feast of St. Mark the Evangelist, should prompt us to read his Gospel, which is the shortest of the four and, I notice, takes up only forty pages in my copy of the New Testament. Perhaps this will start us on regular, preferably daily, reading of the Gospels.

THEY provide the best of spiritual reading. That fact is easily understandable. In the first place, they are God's writings, as well as man's, for they were written under the inspiration of the Holy Ghost. In the second place, they bring us in touch with Our Lord, giving us His own words and showing His own living of the Christian life.

AS WE READ, we hear Him pronounce His Sermon on the Mount, His parables, His discourse on the Bread come down from heaven. His discourse at the Last Supper, and so on. The effect is always to enlighten and move us, and the more we read, the more we learn of Him, are drawn to Him.

—MSGR. JOHN S. KENNEDY

April 26

Mary kept all these things, pondering them in her heart. —Luke 2:19

THE author, Robert Lynd, a Presbyterian, has this passage in his book *Home Life in Ireland:* "If you are in a little town in any part of Ireland — except the northwest — about noon, when the chapel bells ring for the Angelus, you will see all the men suddenly taking off their hats and crossing themselves as they say their mid-day prayers. The world loses its air of work or of commonplace idleness, and the streets take on an intense beauty for the moment as the old people and the young people half hide their eyes and murmur a prayer to the Mother of God ... I confess I like this daily forgetfulness of the world in the world in the middle of the day . . ."

Ah, Mary, pierced with sorrow,
  Remember, reach and save
The soul that comes tomorrow
  Before the God that gave!

Since each was born of woman,
  For each at utter need—
True comrade and true foeman—
  Madonna, intercede!

—*(Rudyard Kipling)*

—FATHER JOHN A. O'BRIEN

April 27

. . . He saw the Spirit of God descending like a dove, and alighting on him, and lo, a voice from heaven, saying, "This is my beloved Son, with whom I am well pleased." —Matthew 3:16-17

PROBABLY the least understood Person in the Trinity is the Holy Spirit, but those who are wise enough to pray to Him receive special strengthening graces, just as the Apostles did on that first Pentecost. It was then Christ sent the Holy Spirit to take His unique role in the Church as a source of holiness, breathing spiritual life into all men, uniting them in faith and love.

FOUR TIMES Scriptures recorded the Holy Spirit appearing under a visible sign: a dove at Christ's baptism; a cloud at His transfiguration; in the breath of Christ when He gave the Apostles the power of forgiving sins, and as the tongues of fire on Pentecost. Though we have no such tangible signs, no less should be our belief in the fruits and gifts of the Holy Spirit.

THOSE FRUITS are: peace, patience, kindness, goodness, faith, modesty and continency. The gifts: wisdom, understanding, counsel, fortitude, knowledge, piety and fear of the Lord. Ask the Holy Spirit for all!

—JO CURTIS DUGAN

April 28

Thy kingdom come, Thy will be done. On earth as it is in heaven. —Matthew 6:10

EACH individual is a little world in himself. No two persons are completely alike nor does anyone completely understand another.

AND YET WE do not live as isolated individuals but we live with others and we influence others or we are influenced by those with whom we live. They shape and change our lives.

THAT IS WHY the spiritual life of the individual must be a happy life. Whether we know it or not, whether we like it or not, we radiate our own personality in various degrees. At times we positively try but even if we at a particular time do not make an effort to influence another, our very presence can have its effect for good or for bad. That is why we are told that the greatest privilege any person can have is to possess the life of God within himself and then "radiate Christ."

—FATHER JAMES D. MORIARTY

April 29

"Blessed are the meek, for they shall inherit the earth."
—Matthew 5:5

H E was an old missionary priest in South Dakota. It was Wednesday morning . . . four below zero. He said Mass at nine o'clock. A dozen Indians attended. Still vested, the beloved priest talked to the crowd around the wood stove.

"GRANDMA, you must have been cold coming to Mass." She was eighty-four and lived in a tent twenty rods from the church. She had two gunny sacks tied around each foot. "Father," she said, "I was not doing this when I was young. Now I must make up for my sins."

THAT NIGHT, the missionary in his bunk in the back of the church, with fur coat, fur cap, felt boots and under two buffalo robes, murmured repeatedly, "I was not doing this when I was young, now I must make up for my sins." He awoke at five, the words for his meditation were on his lips, "I was not doing this when I was young, now I must make up for my sins."
—FATHER TOM MARTIN, S.J.

April 30

"Bless the Lord, all works of the Lord, sing praise to him and highly exalt him for ever. —Daniel 3:35

W HEN we praise the Lord in times of joy and in times of stress, He opens our hearts and minds to a new awareness of His action in our lives. We become more sure of His guidance and more able to cooperate with His grace.

OUR PRAYER LIFE, the inner conversation with God, is constantly growing and deepening. Since it is a matter of learning to listen to the Source and Creator, and to be honest in His presence, it is part of an infinite adventure. None of us can ever be perfect at it. There is always more to learn, more to understand.

AS WE REALIZE that the miracle of Life, and Love, and Truth is, in fact, the Holy Spirit present in the world, we find proof of His love and wisdom everywhere. As we call to the Lord in times of trouble and illness, confusion and efforts to understand, we discover that these too are part of His creation, His loving formation of body and soul. Praise the Lord in all things!
—BETTY WICKHAM

May 1

"Joseph, son of David, do not fear to take Mary your wife. . . ."
—Matthew 1:20

THE ability to work is a gift of God. It is woven into the intrinsic make-up of man.

HOLY MOTHER Church has, during the centuries, honored the spouse of the Blessed Mother with many titles of salutation. Her latest has been St. Joseph the Worker. He, the just man, is the patron of all human beings — men, women, and children — in all walks of life, because all are workers. All, therefore, salute him as their patron.

ONE IS almost sure that the Blessed Mother rejoiced when her Son's Vicar on earth placed the feast of St. Joseph the Worker on the very first day of the month dedicated to her. Great will be our merit when, as real Christian workers, we observe this feast of St. Joseph, spouse of the Blessed Mother and protector of the Sacred Heart.
—BISHOP WILLIAM T. MULLOY, Covington, Kentucky

May 2

The flowers appear on the earth, the time of singing has come. . . .
—The Song of Solomon 2:12

MAY is the month in which nature gathers all her fresh beauty for display. St. John of the Cross says: "The soul being wounded in love by this trace of the beauty of her Beloved which she has known in the creatures, yearns to behold that invisible beauty. . . ." The world should make us yearn for the beauty of God. Especially on a day in May.

HAVE YOU ever considered the fact that God is beautiful? We think of God as just and good and merciful and all-powerful, but *beautiful?*

AND YET none of the lustrous things about us could be clothed with any beauty if it did not come from Him. It follows that He is more beautiful than any of these things which reflect Him. All men yearn for beauty. All men are secretly yearning for God.

WHEN HE had finally found Him, St. Augustine cried out: "Late have I loved thee, O beauty so old and so new."
—MSGR. J. WILLIAM MCKUNE

May 3

Make love your aim, and earnestly desire the spiritual gifts. . . .
—I Corinthians 14:1

IN an ideal home the parents . . . strive to instill into their children from their early years a holy fear of God and true Christian piety. They foster a tender devotion to Jesus, the Blessed Sacrament and the Immaculate Virgin. They teach respect and veneration for holy places and persons.

IN SUCH A HOME the children see in their parents models of upright, industrious and pious living. They see their parents holily loving each other in Our Lord; see them approach the holy sacraments frequently, and not only obey the laws of the Church concerning abstinence and fasting, but also observe the spirit of voluntary Christian mortification.

THEY SEE them pray at home, gathering around them all the family, that common prayer may rise more acceptably to Heaven. They find them compassionate toward the distress of others and see them divide with the poor the much or little they possess. — *(Pope Pius XI)*

—FATHER G. JOSEPH GUSTAFSON, S.S.

May 4

Holy Mary, Mother of God, queen of peace and purity, I dedicate my life to your care, keep me ever safe and free from danger and sin.
—Anonymous

WHAT this month of May will mean to each of us depends upon our awareness of Mary in our lives and our desire to know and love her.

UPON ARISING our thoughts should go out to her with the prayer that we may spend the day in her honor. If possible let us attend Holy Mass and receive Holy Communion.

DURING THE day, even while busy, we can turn our thoughts to Mary, asking her help, sharing with her our sorrows and joys.

IT IS a lovely practice to place flowers before a statue of Our Lady at home. Read about Mary, speak about Mary, seek to imitate Mary. Above all, however, say the daily Rosary to Our Lady. Upon retiring, again commend ourselves to her motherly care. Love of Mary will bring the greatest peace to our lives.

—BISHOP JOHN J. CARBERRY, Lafayette-in-Indiana

May 5

. . . Let all who take refuge in thee rejoice, let them ever sing for joy; and do thou defend them, that those who love thy name may exult in thee. —Psalms 5:11

IN seeking to honor Mary, many will resolve to recite her Rosary with greater devotion, and perhaps daily, if this is not their present custom. Some have thought the Rosary will suffer as a result of the current magnificent liturgical renewal, but the fear is unwarranted. Its recital at Mass, we grant, is properly described as misplaced use of what in itself is splendid prayer.

THE ROSARY is not, as the uninitiated may think, simply a series of Hail Marys set off by Our Fathers. To say it properly one attends to the mysteries attached to the various decades. These are events from the life of Our Lord and His holy Mother.

MARY LEADS us back, as it were, to her life on earth, and bids us gaze upon the mystery of our salvation.Not without reason has the Church recommended the Rosary so earnestly. Its rewards are without number.
—BISHOP JOSEPH M. MARLING, C.PP.S., Jefferson City, Missouri

May 6

"Hail, full of grace, the Lord is with you!" —Luke 1:28

HAIL Mary! At the Annunciation Mary first acted as intercessor between God and man and man and God. Through this act of intercession man was given Christ.

FITTINGLY WE PAY honor to Mary. But the mother wants not glory or honor for herself, rather she wants it for her Son. His will is her will, and His will is that all men in community bring that community to God the Father. One aspect or method of bringing the community to God is the inward betterment of that community. Through the three children at Fatima in 1917, Mary promised help to those people who would observe regular confession, reception of the Eucharist, prayer and meditation on the Mysteries of the Rosary.

TO JESUS THROUGH MARY is the Christian's objective. Together with Mary and all the saints and Jesus we may then approach God. Our community, the Church, the saints, Mary and Joseph and Jesus all are a means to the end, God, our eternal Father.
—ROBERT G. LEE

May 7

Do not boast about tomorrow, for you do not know what a day may bring forth. —Proverbs 27:1

MATURITY in our approach and openness to the Spirit walk hand in hand. The mature man possesses a security in and control of his feelings. He is able to face reality, accept situations as they exist, and turn to other alternatives when a door seems permanently or temporarily closed.

THE PERSON open to God's Spirit working in our lives does not waver with regard to principle. However, he knows that the Lord works in strange ways and may choose a variety of methods to accomplish his purposes. For that reason the open-hearted man fosters within himself an aliveness to promptings from on high.

ST. PAUL followed that path. No longer able to function effectively in Jerusalem, he used Roman confinement as an opportunity to preach the Good News in fresh territory.

—FATHER JOSEPH M. CHAMPLIN

May 8

When I was a child, I spoke like a child, I thought like a child, I reasoned like a child; when I became a man, I gave up childish ways.
—I Corinthians 13:11

THE way to grow — The best way to grow in holiness is to act like Christ. Faith, hope and charity enable us to do so.

FAITH empowers a man to know God in the manner that Christ knows Him. By faith he envisions his final goal; he sees all against the background of eternity, thanks to the divine perspective of reality he shares with Christ.

HOPE is a push Godward. . . . A man could not even begin to aspire to union with God unless he were moved and goaded on to bold and daring aspirations by the virtue of hope.

CHARITY is union with God. It is to love God in the manner that Christ loved His Father. It unites and transforms the person into Christ. Of all the powers possessed by a grace-endowed soul, charity is the greatest. If there is no growth of supernatural life it means there is no love. Lifelessness is lovelessness.

—FATHER ALBERT A. MURRAY, C.S.P.

May 9

Love bears all things, believes all things, hopes all things, endures all things. —I Corinthians 13:7

WE'VE come to use the word charity as simply meaning a good cause. "Will you give to this or that charity?" We're apt to forget that the word charity means love, and love involves a person, in fact, two persons — yourself and another.

A GIFT, whether in cash or kind, isn't charity at all unless you mean it to show your personal love for another, a love that makes demands often far more costly than cash.

OUR BLESSED LORD wasn't a social or political Reformer. He didn't die for the freedom of Israel from Roman oppression. He wasn't concerned with causes, however good, but with people, however bad. He lived and died for persons, weak and wayward. And He gave each of them His sympathy, His understanding, His love; and so He won them over from sin and selfishness to the love of God and of each other.

—FATHER GORDON ALBION

May 10

Hail, Holy Queen, Mother of Mercy, our life, our sweetness, and our hope! To you we cry, poor banished children of Eve; to you we send up our sighs, mourning and weeping in this valley of tears. Turn then, O most gracious advocate, your eyes of mercy toward us, and after this our exile, show unto us the blessed fruit of your womb, Jesus. O clement, O loving, O sweet Virgin Mary. V. Pray for us, O holy Mother of God. R. That we may be made worthy of the promises of Christ.

PERHAPS no prayer to Our Lady is more widely loved and used than the "Salve Regina." What a fitting hymn for May.

SHE IS our Holy Queen because of the impeccable beauty of her life which gave human flesh to the King of Kings. Being the Mother of the Savior, she is also the Mother of Mercy. If Jesus could speak of the Prodigal Son, the wandering sheep and the lost pieces of silver, are we not right in saying that His pity and concern for men was partly a human gift from a compassionate Mother?

IF OUR sins discourage us, if the past rises up to haunt us, if we have no human friend to go to, turn to Our Mother of Mercy.

—FATHER EDWIN R. MCDEVITT, M.M.

May 11

"Here are my mother and my brethren!" —Matthew 12:49

THE United States of America was dedicated to Mary Immaculate in 1846. In times of crisis, a mother rushes to her offspring. Mary often acts as the spiritual mother of many persons in need. She does not need a second request; her spiritual ways are offered immediately to all in our country.

SINCERE humble petitions to Mary, devotions in her honor, and Rosaries offered to receive interceding help are the basic methods used by her adopted children of America to receive her blessings.

OUR LIVES become more meaningful and take on a special purpose when we seek aid and intervention through Mary Immaculate. In the past, she has responded wholeheartedly to the American people's requests. We need her positive attitude to frame new goals and new methods to make our country strong, vibrant, and prosperous.

—JOHN JULIUS FISHER

May 12

". . . Whoever does the will of my Father in heaven is my brother, and sister, and mother." —Matthew 12:50

HAPPINESS is unfailing in the Holy Trinity because love is unfailing too. Love in God is substantial, is infinite. It is the knot between the Father and the Son. It is the Third Person of the Holy Trinity. It is the Holy Spirit.

CHRIST wanted to share His happiness with us by sharing His love with us. It is because He wants us to be permanently happy that He wants us to abide in His love unfailingly.

THERE is a lot of difference between a child being raised with brothers and sisters and a child being raised without them. The first one learns how to love people from being loved by brothers and sisters. This child is happy because it is loved and is able to love. The second one is sad because his life is incomplete.

CHRIST, You are my eldest brother. You love me, I love You. I learn from You how to love my fellow men. You are my perfection. You are my happiness.

—FATHER RICARDO COLIN, M.G.

May 13

"Blessed are the peacemakers, for they shall be called sons of God."
—Matthew 5:9

ONCE the world had hardly ever heard of Fatima. After Our Lady's appearance, however, May 13, 1917, it will never be forgotten.

THERE IS a tie between Fatima and Russia. Our Lady made it very clear in her message: "Russia will be converted and an era of peace will be granted to humanity" if her requests were heard.

AT FATIMA Our Lady asked for the observance of the First Saturday of each month; recitation of the Rosary, meditation on the mysteries of the Rosary, penance and consecration of all to the Immaculate Heart of Mary. On July 7, 1952, Pope Pius XII pronounced these words: "we dedicate and consecrate all peoples of Russia to that same Immaculate Heart."

MAY THE day be hastened when we shall one and all respond to Mary's pleas and true lasting peace be realized in this world. Our Lady of the Rosary of Fatima, pray for us!
—BISHOP JOHN J. CARBERRY, Lafayette-in-Indiana

May 14

And he said to them, "Go into all the world and preach the gospel to the whole creation. . . ." —Mark 16:15

ONE of the greatest miracles of Christianity took place after Jesus returned to the Father. It was on Pentecost. Here were the Apostles, filled with fear after Christ left them, huddling together in the upper room.

THE HOLY SPIRIT, the God of Love, came to them and inspired them so that what Jesus taught now became clear and they had new strength, so, instead of fear, their hearts were filled with extraordinary courage. They went down into the streets of Jerusalem and preached Christ whom the authorities had crucified. They knew it would mean trouble, but now they didn't care. Before, they were afraid the authorities would come and put them in prison or execute them as they had Jesus. But now they spoke out boldly.

WE SHOULD remember that it was probably the prayers of Mary more than anything else that kept the Apostles together before Pentecost.
—FATHER RAWLEY MYERS

May 15

This man went down to his house justified rather than the other; for every one who exalts himself will be humbled, but he who humbles himself will be exalted. —Luke 18:14

LET'S face it. Some people are more gifted by nature than others. To live pleasantly with this fact of life, and to realize that you are not one of those who are so gifted, is plain common sense.

TO LOOK at yourself unafraid, and to acknowledge that you are short of something that makes for leadership — then to stop brooding over it and stop straining against it — is more than common sense. It is a grace. It is a virtue that Our Lord emphasized all through His preaching ministry — the virtue of true humility.

DON'T PUSH up to the head table, He told people at a dinner, lest you get slapped down and then with shame have to take a back seat while all are watching.

HUMILITY does not mean having a poor opinion of yourself. It means making an honest estimate of yourself.

THE VAST number of mental and emotional breakdowns in our world would be cut in half if this simple rule were followed.
—FATHER ALBERT A. MURRAY, C.S.P.

May 16

Mary said, "My soul magnifies the Lord. . . ." —Luke 1:46

MARY'S month is a good time to reflect on what the Blessed Mother should be in our lives.

A HELPER. She certainly listens and lends her assistance now as she once did at Cana in Galilee.

A MODEL. She heard the word of God and kept it.

AN INSPIRATION. She tasted pain and felt swords of sorrow in her heart.

A GOAL. All generations call her blessed and Mary's present joy more than compensates for the crosses she endured on earth.
—FATHER JOSEPH M. CHAMPLIN

May 17

Jesus increased in wisdom and in stature, and in favor with God and man. —Luke 2:52

A T Nazareth, Mary and Joseph taught Jesus to walk and to talk. When He took His first step and said His first clear word, they were delighted. Many a child ends up more learned than his parents, but there is a time when they are his only teachers. So it was with Jesus.

LATER, in His discourses and parables, nothing familiar to His people is missed by Him. He speaks of the wine, the oak, the fig tree, the mustard tree, the sparrow and the dove, the vipers and the wolves. He tells of the reeds and the lilies, the wheat and the cockle, the thorn and the thistles. He takes notice of the seasons, the sun and the rain, the day and the night, the stars and the storms.

NOTHING on which the eye might fall is left unnoticed by His word. And always with the same purpose — to enhance the greatness of the Father in the hearts and minds of His listeners. "Never has man spoken as this man."

—FATHER THOMAS BREW, S.J.

May 18

A faithful man will abound with blessings. —Proverbs 28:20

T HINK and thank — Carved over a mantlepiece in one of our old houses are these words: "Think and Thank."

WHAT a wonderful prescription for life this is! It would truly help us to keep a notebook and write down each day one thing for which we can thank God. At the end of a few months we would see how full our life has been of things for which we can and should say "thank you" to God.

WE SHALL come to see that it is not only our joys and all the glad things in our life for which we should thank Him. If only we will let God take charge of our lives, instead of trying to run them ourselves, we shall find that He can and will bring blessing and even joy out of our sorrow and pain, our hardships, anxieties and failures as well as out of our successes and achievements.

—FATHER ALBERT A. MURRAY, C.S.P.

May 19

Remember, O most holy virgin Mary, that never was it known, that anyone who prayed for your protection, implored your help, and sought your intercession, was left unaided. Inspired with this confidence, I hasten to you, O virgin of virgins, my mother. To you I come; before you I stand, sinful and sorrowful. O mother of the Word Incarnate, despise not my petitions, but in your mercy hear and grant my prayer. Amen.

THE Memorare is a wonderful prayer in honor of Mary. However, have you heard of the Novena of the Memorare? It is very simple — nine Memorare *each* day for *nine* days. These can be brought very easily into every day if we will plan to recite the Memorare three times in the morning, noon, and evening.

IT IS not difficult either to keep track of the days of the Memorare Novena. Let the Novena begin on the first day of the month and end on the ninth.

LET US make the Novena for the intention to grow in the knowledge and love of Mary. We will be amazed at the results.
— BISHOP JOHN J. CARBERRY, Lafayette-in-Indiana

May 20

And his mother said to him, "Son why have you treated us so? Behold, your father and I have been looking for you anxiously."
—Luke 2:48

WE must never think that the Blessed Virgin had an easy life. If anything is clear in the Gospels, it is that the Blessed Virgin's condition, as far as her experience went, was very similar to ours; she had to *work out* her salvation.

SHE ENJOYED NO privileges that would make things easier. The apparently "harsh" words which Our Lord addressed to her were obviously intended to show that her role as His Mother did not exempt her from playing the normal part of a pilgrim on earth hoping for the happiness of heaven.

"DID YOU not know that I must be about my Father's business?" is a clear statement, setting the record straight.

THIS MUST have been a little hard for Mary to understand. It must have been hard for her to "find her place" in Our Lord's life. But she met the problem with courage, keeping "all these things in her heart."

—MSGR. J. WILLIAM MCKUNE

May 21

For the gifts and the call of God are irrevocable. —Romans 11:29

VOCATION is a mysterious word. One thing for sure: everybody has one. The priest . . . the Sister . . . the monk . . . the mother and father . . . the dedicated doctor and nurse. . . . We can't forget the vocation of the invalid — silent and seemingly withdrawn from society . . . the retarded, objects of devoted care . . . the aged, whose time of usefulness is apparently past.

EACH one of us, indeed, is "set apart" for a work "to which the Lord has called us." This may become evident in our earliest years. Some of us may grope in darkness for the better part of a lifetime. We will be judged on our attempt to do God's will.

JESUS, whether my task is evident and clear or puzzling and hidden, give me this confidence!

—DIANNE RUSSELL

May 22

The angel of the Lord declared unto Mary,
R. *And she conceived by the Holy Spirit. / Hail Mary, etc.*
V. *Behold the handmaid of the Lord.*
R. *Be it done unto me according to your word. / Hail Mary, etc.*
V. *And the Word was made flesh*
R. *And dwelt among us. / Hail Mary, etc.*
V. *Pray for us, O holy Mother of God.*
R. *That we may be made worthy of the promises of Christ.*
Let us pray. *Pour forth, we beseech You, O Lord, Your grace into our hearts, that as we have known the incarnation of Christ, Your Son, by the message of an angel, so by His passion and cross we may be brought to the glory of His resurrection. Through the same Christ our Lord. Amen.*

AMONG the treasures of Catholic devotion is certainly the Angelus. This practice of commemorating the Incarnation morning, noon, and evening, and thus honoring the Savior and His Blessed Mother, can be traced to the Middle Ages. References to it in literature and art have been abundant.

IF WE PAUSE at the appointed time each day to relive, as it were, the Annunciation, greeting Jesus and Mary, it will take us away from the busy world about us just long enough to deepen our spiritual life, and to gain a great blessing.

—BISHOP JOSEPH M. MARLING, C.PP.S., Jefferson City, Missouri

May 23

. . . They see your reverent and chaste behavior. —I Peter 3:2

CONJUGAL chastity has always been part of married life in the Church. This sacredness has been heralded by Holy Mary, Mother Most Chaste. The sacred purpose of a Catholic marriage is to be faithful to spouse and to cooperate with God in the propagation of the human race. This always has been a tenet of the Church.

THE POISONS of unfaithfulness, abuse, and sexual deviation have caused the marriage institution to suffer. Many partners in marriage, as well as their children, have experienced the pains and hardships created by occasional sins that would cause gaps and chasms in spiritual lives.

WHEN PETITIONED, Mother Most Chaste has interceded for many. Needful persons, who by prayers and devotions, have found new hope by seeking Mary's help. Once more, the presence of God entered their married life and love began to blossom again.

—JOHN JULIUS FISHER

May 24

Let those who suffer according to God's will do right and entrust their souls to a faithful Creator. —I Peter 4:19

MARY, who must have had knowledge of the events which marked the start of Jesus' passion, witnessed the carrying of the cross and the crucifixion. And the sword foretold by Simeon was deep in her heart.

ACCORDING to a time-honored tradition, she met Jesus along the path of the most painful way of a cross in the history of human cruelty and moral perversity. While the soldiers prodded Him along the 1,000-odd yard way, she offered Him the sympathy of her tears and the strength of her presence.

LONG BEFORE this happened, Mary had surrendered Jesus to the performance of the Father's will. She supported Him in that during His public ministry. Now, at the end, she co-offered Him, with herself, for the final accomplishment of the divine saving will.

—FATHER FELICIAN A. FOY, O.F.M.

May 25

He said to the disciple, "Behold, your mother!" And from that hour the disciple took her to his own home. —John 19:27

WE know that Mary is the Mother of Our Lord. But how can we say that she is our mother? Sometimes you hear the answer: When Our Lord was on the cross, He said to St. John, "Behold your mother," and that meant that He was giving His mother to be the mother of us all.

BUT PEOPLE with literal minds may say: No. Our Lord was providing for the care and support of His mother by "giving" her to St. John. Nothing is said about giving her to us.

BUT MARY is our mother because in a sense, *everything* of Christ's is ours.

HE HAD created the universe long before, knowing that He was to become part of it. He entered it by means of Mary. Very well. If she was the instrument by which He took over His world, then she is a Source of the life He brings with Him.

—MSGR. J. WILLIAM MCKUNE

May 26

He who disciplines his son will profit by him, and will boast of him among his acquaintances. —Sirach 30:2

ST. Philip Neri can be a source of inspiration for all of us for his work was chiefly among young boys who were neglected. We learn from St. Philip that juvenile delinquency is not new to the Church. It existed even in his day. He, however, did something to counteract the dangers.

ST. PHILIP started with prayer, which was a daily source of strength and zeal for him. Then he provided for the education of these young boys and planned their leisure time. "Amuse yourself, but do not offend God" was a directive for their daily life.

AS A CATHOLIC and as a citizen what have I done for the neglected young boys and girls of my neighborhood? Have I really shown my zeal to provide a place of play and wholesome recreation for them?

—BISHOP WILLIAM T. MULLOY, Covington, Kentucky

May 27

Hail Mary, full of grace, the Lord is with you; blessed are you among women, and blessed is the fruit of your womb, Jesus. Holy Mary, Mother of God, pray for us sinners, now and at the hour of our death. Amen.

S T. Louis De Montfort has listed the ten principal virtues of Mary: her profound humility, her lively faith, her blind obedience, her continual mental prayer, her mortification in all things, her divine purity, her ardent charity, her heroic patience, her angelic sweetness and her divine wisdom.

THE VERY reading of these virtues gives rise to a certain peace of soul, a desire for imitation, a yearning to put into practice even just one of them.

WHERE SHALL we begin? Let us ask her to show us the way. Very prayerfully and sincerely turn to Our Lady as to a loving Mother and select one of these virtues at a time for practice and development in our souls.

—BISHOP JOHN J. CARBERRY, Lafayette-in-Indiana

May 28

. . . I went with the throng, and led them in procession to the house of God, with glad shouts and songs of thanksgiving. —Psalms 42:4

W HEN we go to church we should not be bothered by little matters. We shouldn't be put off by externals. The main thing is that Christ is there. The church may not be very beautiful, the servers at Mass may be gawky, the priest might be awkward. But Christ is there. And if we are with Him, how little these other things really matter. We do hope, of course, that the liturgy is not full of stunts, but even these distractions, though disconcerting, should never take us away from the tremendous fact that we are with Christ.

WE SHOULD turn our full attention to Our Lord and praise Him from our hearts just as spontaneously as a song is sung by a lark or fragrance comes from a flower. Of all places, surely in church we should not be preoccupied with trivia. Just as if we had seen Him in Palestine we could not have taken our eyes off Him as He spoke, so our faith tells us Jesus is here with us also. And we should speak to Him in prayer. Jesus said, "My house is a house of prayer."

AND WE SAY to Him, "All praise to you, Lord God. Honor and glory forever."

—FATHER RAWLEY MYERS

May 29

O Queen of heaven, rejoice! Alleluia.
For He whom you merited to bear, Alleluia,
Has arisen, as He said. Alleluia.
Pray for us to God. Alleluia.
V. *Rejoice and be glad, O Virgin Mary, Alleluia.*
R. *For the Lord has risen indeed. Alleluia.*
Let us pray. *O God, who through the resurrection of Your Son, our Lord Jesus Christ, willed to fill the world with joy, grant, we beseech You, that through His Virgin Mother, Mary, we may come to the joys of everlasting life. Through the same Christ our Lord. Amen.*

THE Documents of Vatican Council II contain these words on Mary, the Mother of God.

". . . For Mary figured profoundly in the history of salvation and in a certain way unites and mirrors within herself the central truths of the faith. Hence when she is being preached and venerated, she summons the faithful to her Son and His sacrifice, and to love for the Father. Seeking after the glory of Christ, the Church becomes more like her exalted model, and continually progresses in faith, hope, and charity, searching out and doing the will of God in all things. Hence the Church in her apostolic work also rightly looks to her who brought forth Christ, conceived by the Holy Spirit and born of the Virgin, so that through the Church Christ may be born and grow in the hearts of the faithful also. The Virgin Mary in her own life lived an example of that maternal love by which all should be fittingly animated who cooperate in the apostolic mission of the Church on behalf of the rebirth of men" (*Dogmatic Constitution on the Church*, No. 65).

—FATHER FELICIAN A. FOY, O.F.M.

May 30

Greater love has no man than this, that a man lay down his life for his friends. —John 15:13

ON Memorial Day we honor all those who gave their lives in the defense of our country. In parades and the placing of wreaths upon graves of fallen patriots we symbolize our hope and faith that they did not die in vain. We silently thank them for their greatest of gifts to men, their very lives.

THE YOUNG LIVES GIVEN reminds us of a young life given two thousand years ago that men may come to love one another.

—ROBERT G. LEE

To venerate Mary correctly means to acknowledge her Son, for she is the Mother of God. To love her means to love Jesus, for she is always the Mother of Jesus. To pray to our Lady means not to substitute her for Christ, but to glorify her Son who desires us to have loving confidence in His Saints, especially in His Mother. To imitate the "faithful Virgin" means to keep her Son's commandments.

—Behold Your Mother 4:82

TODAY we end the month of May by honoring Mary as we commemorate her visit to Elizabeth which provides us with many lessons. Mary goes out of her way to help another. Do we? Mary spreads the good news of salvation. Do we? John stirs in the womb of Elizabeth because he senses the presence of God in Mary. Do people have the same reaction to us?

MARY stands as a real woman of faith, a woman who was undaunted by consistently negative circumstances in her life. She rose above every limitation and became a truly liberated woman not through egocentricity, self-assertion or a petty clinging to personal rights but by giving herself over totally to God.

THE GOSPELS only give us one instance of Mary's giving directives but that one is sufficient: "Do whatever He tells you" (John 2:5). That one injunction is a task of a lifetime. She excelled in taking her own advice and that is why every generation of Christians has fulfilled her prophecy by calling her "blessed."

—REV. MR. PETER M. STRAVINSKAS

June 1

"He who is mighty has done great things for me, and holy is his name." —Luke 1:49

MAY, Mary's month, is followed by the month dedicated to the Sacred Heart of Jesus. Thus it should be, for Mary leads to Jesus. That is her role.

IF IN THE MONTH of May we gave special thoughts to our Blessed Mother, then it will not be difficult to turn our thoughts to the Sacred Heart in June. For devotion to Mary, if it is true, if it does her honor, if it is pleasing to her, will not stop with her.

IN THE GOSPEL Mary's role is clearly indicated. She is mentioned only a few times, and then only in her relation to her Son. At Bethlehem she "brought forth her first born" and presented Him to Shepherd and Magi. At Cana she introduced Him to the public. On Calvary she suffered with Him and she offered with Him.

AT MARY'S side we shall learn what it means to love the Sacred Heart.

—BISHOP HENRY A. PINGER, O.F.M., Chowtsun, China

June 2

. . . I have loved you with an everlasting love; therefore I have continued my faithfulness to you. —Jeremiah 31:3

DIGESTS are very popular nowadays. But the greatest of them all is the one that tells at a glance the story of God's love. It is none other than the transpierced Heart of Jesus, surrounded by thorns, with a cross in the midst of flames.

DURING THIS month of June frequently read this story in the "book of the Sacred Heart." Do it right now. Look at an image of the Sacred Heart. Here is the story it tells.

IT BEGINS with a prologue: "I have loved you with an everlasting love," *(Jeremiah 31:3)*.

THE FIRST chapter: the Incarnation. "See, how I have loved you!"

THE SECOND chapter: the Passion. "See how very much I have loved you!"

THE THIRD chapter: the Eucharist. "See, O see how I have loved you!"

—FATHER FRANCIS LARKIN, SS.CC.

June 3

". . . I have baptized you with water; but he will baptize you with the Holy Spirit." —Mark 1:8

THE Holy Spirit transformed Christ at the resurrection into the glorified Lord of the universe, radiant with divine life and holiness. We see in the glorification of Christ the power of the Spirit of God. He marked Jesus with holiness from the beginning of His earthly life. But in the risen life of Our Lord we see even more glorious effects of the Spirit.

THE SPIRIT first comes to us in baptism and again in confirmation. He dwells within us, the gift of the risen Jesus. Through His gentle urgings we are led to live the Christian life, to be more like Jesus and to show forth His love in the world. If we are faithful, He will lead us to glory.

BUT WE ALL, with faces unveiled, reflecting as in a mirror the glory of the Lord, are being transformed into His very image from glory to glory as through the Spirit of the Lord.

—FATHER KEVIN A. LYNCH, C.S.P.

June 4

He died for all, that those who live might live no longer for themselves but for him who for their sake died and was raised.
—2 Corinthians 5:15

JUNE is, for many, the most beautiful month of the year. It has weather, anniversaries of weddings, graduations and, for many in the religious life, fond memories of ordinations, ceremonies of vows.

JUNE is commonly dedicated to the Sacred Heart and few devotions have the warmth and appeal of motivation, prayers and practice involved in the manifestation of Christ's great love for us and our determination to catch some of His spirit.

IN SPANISH Catholic culture the word "simpatico" is often identified with devotion to the Sacred Heart; sympathy is not the best translation for an ideal that includes forgiveness, a refusal to remember slights that we have suffered; "simpatico" means a positive charity, a warmth and genuine interest in another. Whatever our resolutions in the past, we can, during June, make a little stronger effort to reflect the love that the Sacred Heart has for us.

—FATHER ROBERT E. SHERIDAN, M.M.

June 5

Sing praises to the Lord, O you his saints, and give thanks to his holy name. —Psalms 30:4

THE saint commemorated today has an interesting and appropriate name. He was baptized Winfrid but is much better known as Boniface. The word means a doer of good, not the same as a "do-gooder." The good he did is the story of his life as a missionary reformer, bishop and martyr in a rough period of Church history.

ONE REASON for honoring the saints is that they always give us ordinary Christians an extraordinary example of Christian life.

IT IS OFTEN SAID, but not too often appreciated, that the home is the first school of virtue. It is there that we see for the first time how people act toward God and toward each other. It is there, in fact, that we get our first rudimentary lesson in what is good and what is bad. Usually it stays with us.
—BISHOP LEO A. PURSLEY, Fort Wayne-South Bend, Indiana

June 6

O taste and see that the Lord is good! —Psalms 34:8

WHAT happened at Paray-le-Monial? In 1673 Our Blessed Lord appeared to a humble nun in the chapel of the Visitation convent. The name of this favored religious was Margaret Mary Alacoque. Later she was to be canonized as St. Margaret Mary. More than seventy times before her death St. Margaret Mary was to receive apparitions and revelations from the Sacred Heart.

IN FOUR GREAT revelations He was to give to the world through her His call to love, consecration, reparation and confidence. As a matter of fact Jesus Christ started in this hidden-away place a revolution of Divine Love in the modern world. No wonder that Bishop Bougaud, the biographer of St. Margaret Mary, and Father Bainvel, the historian of this devotion, both say that nothing more important has happened since the day of Pentecost. According to one expert Paray-le-Monial is the most important place in Christendom, after the holy places in Palestine.
—FATHER EUGENE P. MURPHY, S.J.

June 7

And he went about all Galilee, teaching . . . and preaching the gospel . . .
and healing every disease and every infirmity among the people.
—Matthew 4:23

THE healing of a crippled man by St. Peter in the name and by the power of Jesus was one of many signs and wonders performed by the Apostles. All of them happened in virtue of divine power working through the intervention of human agents.

HEALINGS in our day remain a manifestation of divine compassion: spiritual healing of the wounds of sin through the ministry of a priest in the Sacrament of Reconciliation; fraternal healing of misunderstanding, rancor and injustice through reconciling action between one person and another; healing in wider spheres of society through the agency of people seeking to establish or restore the order of God's kingdom in the world of men.

JESUS has healed many people because of their faith, personally during His own time on earth and, since then, through the mediation of people. We can try to be agents of healing by becoming instruments of His peace.
—FATHER FELICIAN A. FOY, O.F.M.

June 8

To one is given through the Spirit the utterance of wisdom. . . .
—I Corinthians 12:8

"FROM these you can learn the wisdom that leads to salvation through faith in Christ Jesus." We are so used to hearing television commercials promise the moon through this or that product that we become wary and skeptical in our approach. That is reasonable enough, but when St. Paul wrote the above sentence he was not writing about health foods.

HE WAS talking about a book most of us have on a shelf somewhere — the Holy Scriptures. He was writing to advise Timothy on how to set about his life-project.

THE COUNCIL was even stronger on the subject: "For in the sacred books, the Father who is in heaven meets his children with great love and speaks with them; and the force and power in the word of God is so great that it remains the support and energy of the Church, the strength of faith for her sons, the food of the soul, the pure and perennial source of spiritual life."
—MSGR. PETER COUGHLAN

June 9

"Blessed is the womb that bore you. ..." But he said, "Blessed rather are those who hear the word of God and keep it!"
—Luke 11:27-28

BLESSEDNESS is the condition of a person who is found holy in the sight of God. Exact synonyms for blessedness are holiness and sanctity.

A WOMAN once interrupted one of Christ's sermons to praise Him by noting that the Mother of Christ must have indeed been a holy, saintly woman. Our Lord underscored her understatement, "What you say is very true, but also they are holy who hear the word of God and keep it." Here is the secret of Mary's sanctity. Here is the secret of sanctity itself — to hear the word of God; to hear the teaching of Christ and then to live what He taught fully.

THE WHOLE of the Word of God teaches us to imitate the self-sacrificing love of Christ. Our whole duty as followers of Christ is to be spent in loving God and loving men in a kind of love that seeks to enrich, to aid, to pour out all blessings on another. It is the truly outgoing love of Christ, never satisfied until we see those we love in the bliss of heaven.

—FATHER G. JOSEPH GUSTAFSON, S.S.

June 10

Happy is he . . . whose hope is in the Lord his God. . . .
—Psalms 146:5

HOPE means you have confidence that life is good. Hope is not blind, of course to the obstacles lying in the way of accomplishing Christian ideals. It sees clearly where the problems lie.

BUT HOPE SEES power for good in God who supports man. God's design comes to pass through sorrow as through joy, with joy as the ultimate meaning of it all, somehow and sometime to be made evident.

IT IS NOT that hope ceases all effort in some carefree reliance on God alone. Self too is a tool of hope. One sees oneself as the instrument of God, a reason for optimism, sure that God's purposes will be attained in the end, and in part at least through me. I must work, therefore, as though all depended on me. I must pray and rely, as though all depended on God.

—FATHER GILBERT ROXBURGH, O.P.

June 11

"The Father of mercies comforts us in all our afflictions and thus enables us to comfort those who are in any trouble."
—2 Corinthians 1:4

THERE is much sorrow in this world, and it does no good to put the thought of it out of our minds. Among other reasons that sorrow exists is for the purpose of keeping us from losing our hearts in this world and forgetting that there is another world where "every tear will be wiped away."

GOD CAN console the sorrowing by inward grace but it is good for us to think of ourselves as His messengers of consolation. Even when we cannot relieve the cause of suffering it helps people to know that others care for them.

HOW MANY may be waiting for a word of consolation, the sick, shut-ins, prisoners, the poor, the old, the sick — and if we do not bring it, who will? Blessed are the sorrowing; they shall be consoled — by us.
—FATHER VINCENT P. MALLON, M.M.

June 12

Attend to the public reading of scripture, to preaching, to teaching.
—I Timothy 4:13

PONDER these words of Alfonso Rodriguez whose writings have done so much to form the Catholic man.

"READING is the sister of prayer and a great help to it. That is why the Apostle St. Paul advises his disciple Timothy that he should give reading his attention. Spiritual reading is of such great importance for him who is trying to serve God that St. Athanasius says in an exhortation he makes to his religious: 'You will not see anyone who is really striving after his advancement who is not given to spiritual reading, and as to him who neglects it, the fact will soon be observable in his progress.'

"ST. JEROME, in his letter to Eustochium, strongly recommends her to devote herself to this holy reading, saying: 'Take your sleep reading, and when, overcome by sleep, you begin to nod, let your head fall on the sacred book.' "

OR AS St. Ambrose said, "When we read, we listen to God."
—FATHER G. JOSEPH GUSTAFSON, S.S.

June 13

"Rejoice with me, for I have found my sheep which was lost."
                                                          —Luke 15:6

A SISTER teaching the second grade once interrupted her story
of how Jesus was lost in the temple at the age of twelve, with
the question, "What do you think Mary and Joseph did when they
couldn't find Jesus?"

WITHOUT hesitation little Louis volunteered, "I think they
knelt down and said a prayer to St. Anthony!"

IT IS IN this capacity of finding whatever is lost that St.
Anthony is best known, although this came about unintentionally.
With no printing press, handwriting on parchment was the chief
method of preserving facts from one generation to the next. The life
of St. Anthony was thus recorded, and the paper folded a number of
times. Over the years, it was read and refolded many times. The
words on the creases could not be deciphered and the transcriber
thought it was "finder of lost objects," and wrote it thus. Anthony,
of course, is as good as his title.

GOOD St. Anthony, intercede for me that, with you, I may find
heaven as well as the things that lead there.

                                          —THERESITA POLZIN

June 14

*Bless the Lord, stars of heaven, sing praise to him and highly exalt
him for ever.*   —Daniel 3:41

H AVE you ever seen a falling star, or watched a penny sink to
the bottom of the well? Have you ever looked heavenward on
a clear June evening and wondered if the moon could speak to the
sun? Have you ever made a wish and dreamed that it came true? We
have all had experiences similar to these, but I wonder if we all
appreciated them in the same way . . . in relation to God.

ONE OF the greatest gifts which God has given mankind is the
gift of imagining — of seeing things which do not as yet exist — of
hearing things which no one else had heard. As Christians it is our
duty to exercise and bring to fruition the fullness of this gift.

WE HAVE to develop a sense of the beautiful. A sense of the
holy. God is truth, goodness and beauty and if we fail to appreciate
the last of these, we will also fail in love.

                                          — T. TIMOTHY DELANEY

June 15

. . . Let us not love in word or speech but in deed and in truth.
—I John 3:18

" **W** E are to love one another" (1 John 3:11) to find the real spiritual meaning of the power of love. This great magnificent force is present in our heart, mind and soul—a gift of the Father. Love is meant for all God's children.

JESUS CHRIST, the only begotten Son of God, is the visible grand example of total love of Father and all the Father's children. Jesus led a life of total surrender to the love that is manifested by the Father.

JESUS taught us to live in peace with all men, to be pure, to try to understand the will of the Father no matter how difficult it may seem. He taught, that your enemies are your brothers in Christ, so they are part of God's Family.

O GOD, let me be an instrument of Your love. Let me give mercy and understanding to all that seek it, whether it be friend or foe.

—JOHN JULIUS FISHER

June 16

Let your fountain be blessed, and rejoice in the wife of your youth.
—Proverbs 5:18

T HE prayers of the marriage ceremony are perhaps the most beautiful to be found anywhere. Re-reading these prayers, even years after one has been married, can bring fresh insights into just what marriage is.

THE PRAYERS are not lofty and complicated. They are down to earth and strikingly realistic. One of the finest prayers asks that the couple may always have true friends to stand by them both in joy and in sorrow. It asks that the couple respond to people who come to them in need. It hopes that happiness and satisfaction may be found in their work, and that daily problems will not cause them undue anxiety.

THESE ARE the wishes that make marriage more than the cohabitation of strangers. To be satisfied with simple things, to answer the pleas of the needy, to cherish the friendship of others: this is the stuff of which love is made.

—JAMES M. SULLIVAN, M.M.

June 17

. . . Serving the Lord with all humility and with tears and trials which befell me. . . . —Acts 20:19

S T. Francis de Sales has been quoted as writing: "Humility which does not produce generosity is indubitably false." Humility is commonly referred to as the basis of solid spiritual structuring while generosity is established as necessary for beginners in a life of ultimate perfection.

HUMILITY has been associated with saints who accomplished great good for God and His Church. Many founders of religious communities could be named who suffered major humiliations before their works where blessed by God. When one realizes that humility scourges the evil while pride scourges our Savior we can understand the value of accepting the one virtue that is not only truth but the foundation of a life erected on the most solid of foundations.

THERE ARE tests and tests to discern genuine humility but it remained for St. Francis de Sales to emphasize the validity of the thesis that "humility which does not produce generosity is indubitably false."

—FATHER ROBERT E. SHERIDAN

June 18

As Jesus passed . . . he saw a man called Matthew sitting at the tax office; and he said to him, "Follow me." And he rose and followed him. —Matthew 9:9

S OMEONE has said that there are three inescapable evils in life: death, taxes and TV commercials. It is likely that taxes bother most people more than the other two. Accordingly, tax collectors are not popular as such, however agreeable they may be as persons.

ST. MATTHEW was a tax collector. He was guilty by association of being also a sinner. But Our Lord chose him to be an Apostle, as the Gospel tells us.

WE CAN UNDERSTAND why the Jews held tax collectors in such contempt. They were hired agents of pagan Rome and some of them cheated the taxpayer to enrich themselves. Our Lord does not deny the facts, but He gives no comfort to the self-righteous. He proclaims His mission of mercy to all sinners, especially those who are more concerned about the sins of others than their own.

—BISHOP LEO A. PURSLEY, Fort Wayne-South Bend, Indiana

June 19

Those who received his word were baptized, and there were added that day about three thousand souls. —Acts 2:41

THE term Lay Apostolate may be new in our time, but not new is the apostolate carried on by the laity.

THE FIRST converts on the first Pentecost were from many parts of the world. They carried with them their faith, treasured it, preserved it at great sacrifice, and propagated it. In Rome the Church could not have survived the centuries of persecution, much less could there have been any growth without the apostolate of the laity.

TIME and circumstances determine the method, but the basis remains the same. We can radiate love only if our hearts are afire with love. We can dispel the darkness of unbelief only if our words and actions reflect the light of faith. Love and faith will remain strong when constantly nourished by the love of the Heart that is all love, and the light which is the Light of the world.

—BISHOP HENRY A. PINGER, O.F.M., Chowtsun, China

June 20

"Lord, he whom you love is ill." —John 11:3

ONE of the most human stories in the Gospel is the friendship of Jesus for Lazarus, Martha and Mary. This family lived in Bethany, not far from Jerusalem. Frequently Our Lord stayed with His friends, and it was on one of these visits, that Martha complained to Jesus, Who didn't seem to be concerned that Mary wasn't helping her prepare the meal.

JESUS WEPT when Lazarus died, and raised His friend from the dead. Mary had already been raised from the mire of sin and she was privileged to stand at the foot of the Cross near His Mother.

SOMETIMES we envy this family for having had Our Lord as a special friend. But families that have enthroned the Sacred Heart in their homes, say they have experienced the hidden presence of Jesus, and that He has been a true Friend in their hour of need.

—FATHER FRANCIS LARKIN, SS.CC.

June 21

O God, from my youth you have taught me, and I still proclaim your wondrous deeds. —Psalms 71:17

S T. Aloysius Gonzaga was one of the Church's noblest teen-agers! He was handsome, lovable, devout, studious, quiet, and recollected. His life from his First Communion — from the hand of St. Charles Borromeo who was visiting the family — was a triumph of the Spirit at work within him. What can be done with the proper dispositions and effort!

ST. ALOYSIUS was practical and brave in his charity; in fact he was heroic. He was quiet but he did not stand back. He gave his life in earliest manhood serving the sick in an epidemic in Rome. The saying, "Good makes no noise, and noise makes no good" could have been written of him.

OUR ALTAR BOYS follow their patrons, Saints Aloysius and Tarcisius the martyr, to show us our teen-agers can still be devout, quiet, and sacrificing.

—FATHER CONRAD LOUIS, O.S.B.

June 22

As the Father has loved me, so have I loved you; abide in my love. —John 15:9

T HE feast of the Sacred Heart of Jesus is the celebration of the love that God has for mankind, displayed to the full in the love of the Heart of Christ. "No one has ever seen God; the only Son, who is in the bosom of the Father, he has made him known" (John 1:18).

IT IS through knowing and experiencing the breadth and length and height and depth of Christ's love that we can attain the fullness of God's gifts to us. God has many claims on us, many titles to our complete loyalty. Yet He has the prophet Hosea tell us that He prefers to treat His people (Ephraim) as a favorite child. He uses only those restraints that are necessary to keep him from falling as he tries to learn to walk.

THE FATHER could not love the Son more than He does. Yet He gave Him up for us. And the Son came gladly down to earth for us men and for our salvation. "Greater love has no man than this, that a man lay down his life for his friends" (John 15:13).

—FATHER VINCENT P. MALLON, M.M.

June 23

". . . May her Rosary be found in the hands of all. May she gather together small groups or great multitudes of Christ's faithful in churches, in homes, in hospitals, and in prisons, to sing her praises."
—Pope Pius XII

THE Commemoration of the Immaculate Heart of Mary, now an optional memorial, was originally ordered by Pope Pius XII, May 4, 1944, for observance throughout the Church in order to obtain Mary's intercession for "peace among nations, freedom for the Church, the conversion of sinners, the love of purity and the practice of virtue." Two years earlier, the Holy Father consecrated all peoples to Mary under the title of her Immaculate Heart.

THE INTENTIONS stated by the Pope were related to those suggested by Mary during appearances to two French children at LaSalette in 1846, to St. Bernadette at Lourdes in 1858, and to three Portuguese children at Fatima in 1917. The urgency of the intentions, which have been recommended in numerous pastoral statements, is undeniable.
—FATHER FELICIAN A. FOY, O.F.M.

June 24

There was a man sent from God, whose name was John.
—John 1:6

THE Church focuses today on the birth of that rather awesome figure, John the Baptist. All we know about him was that "the hand of the Lord was with him" and that "he lived out in the wilderness" until the day he began to preach openly that Christ was coming.

THERE ARE not many whose vocation in life stands out with such stark clarity, yet each of us has a personal vocation. Little though we know of John the Baptist, we at least see the call of God realized in every aspect of his life. The responsorial psalm says: "O Lord, you have probed me and you know me; you know when I sit and when I stand; you understand my thoughts from afar." This is true not only of John but of each of us.

THE VATICAN COUNCIL stated unequivocally: "It is evident that all the faithful of Christ of whatever rank or status are called to the fullness of Christian life and to the perfection of charity." Here is our call, and it is something unique to each of us.
—MSGR. PETER COUGHLAN

June 25

"As soon as its branch becomes tender and puts forth its leaves, you know that summer is near." —Matthew 24:32

IT'S summer. It is white, puffy clouds hanging loosely over a field of yellow and green. It is bicycle spokes with long red balloons attached; slender country roads winding through the fields of wheat; and the green smell of freshly cut grass preceded by the roar of the lawn mower's engine.

SUMMER is a lot of things. The sounds, sights and feelings of the summer months say something different to all of us, but in all of these various explosions of the season, we find the work of God. In the warmth of the summer sun we find the comfort of leisure's prayer. In the flower which grows through the rock we are able to find the significance of the resurrection. In the coolness of a June night we find the peace which is God's gift to us.

WITH summer also comes the rain. But those rainy hours seem so much happier as long as we realize that without them there would be no trees, indeed, no summer. We should celebrate rain. We should celebrate sun. We should celebrate June as a gift to us from God.

—T. TIMOTHY DELANEY

June 26

When you pray, say: "Father, hallowed be thy name. Thy kingdom come. Give us each day our daily bread; and forgive us our sins, for we ourselves forgive every one who is indebted to us; and lead us not into temptation." —Luke 11:2-4

HAVE you ever sat down and made an accounting of how you spent a day or a week? Many of us make an annual retreat of a few days or even a week. On your next spiritual retreat make a tally of the time spent in prayer.

THE HARD truth is that we spend too little time opening our hearts to our Father in prayer and listening in silence as He answers. With all His activities Jesus still found time for prayer — in the desert, alone on the mountain, in the Garden of Gethsemani.

HE PRAYED, too, before raising Lazarus and at the Last Supper. Like Jesus we should pray always.

—FATHER KEVIN A. LYNCH, C.S.P.

June 27

"This cup which is poured out for you is the new covenant in my blood." —Luke 22:17

JUST as bread has its special meaning, so has wine. "The fruit of the vine," as it is called, symbolizes suffering and hardships, for the process by which grapes are changed into pure Mass wine is one of destruction of the grape. The fruit must be pressed together and left to ferment in the darkness until its original form and taste are destroyed. Only when it surrenders its identity completely can it come forth worthy of becoming the living Blood of Jesus in the Eucharist.

AT THE Offertory of the Mass, when the wine is offered, we, too, join our sufferings and hardships with this external gift, so that in the Consecration these will be changed with the wine into Jesus.

THUS the reason for Jesus' choice of bread and wine was that these two together signify our whole lives: our work and daily living, plus our sufferings and hardships.

DEAR LORD, accept me in my daily life with the bread and wine in the Offertory. Change me into Yourself, as You change these gifts which symbolize me.

—THERESITA POLZIN

June 28

We are his workmanship, created in Christ Jesus for good works, which God prepared beforehand, that we should walk in them.
—Ephesians 2:10

JESUS, because He is our Savior, demands that we be filled with a real zeal for souls. Did He not say, "I am come to cast fire on the earth and what would I but that it be enkindled?" In other words, He needs us to start and spread the conflagration of divine love which is this "fire on the earth." When we use the simple little ejaculation "Heart of Jesus, burning with love of me, enkindle my heart with love of Thee" we are asking for a consuming zeal for souls.

THERE COMES a time in the life of every Catholic when he or she realizes that money, fame, friends, pleasure, travel, influence are not the things that count — but souls. It is souls that matter. We must be other Francis Xaviers if our contribution to mankind means anything — and he cried out, "Lord, give me souls, give me souls."

—FATHER EUGENE P. MURPHY, S.J.

June 29

Humble yourselves before the Lord and he will exalt you.

—James 4:10

"BE Children of the Church, Be Children of the Church," were the dying words of the newly canonized American Saint — Elizabeth Seton. Both Saints Peter and Paul were early-day leaders of Christ's Church — they truly were among the first children of the Church.

TODAY we need more leaders in the Church who are willing to humble themselves to be regarded as "little children" in the service of others. When the Apostles were arguing among themselves about who was the greatest, Christ reminded them that the greatest was the servant of all. But how often we forget that it is in service to others that we really achieve the greatness that God intended for us.

SERVICE requires humility in our relationships with others. As we serve, let us try to remember: "Not my will, but Thy will be done."

—MARGARET H. MALSAM

June 30

The eyes of the Lord are upon the righteous, and his ears are open to their prayer. —I Peter 3:12

WE are all reasonably concerned these days. A President of the United States, or Congress, may have to make critical decisions which seriously endanger our future. How wise, then, to look at things from the eternal point of view, as did Brother Giles, an intimate of St. Francis of Assisi.

A CERTAIN Brother asked Brother Giles, saying: "Father, if great adversities or tribulations should fall in our time, what should we do then?" And Brother Giles replied:

"MY BROTHER, I would have thee know that if the Lord were to rain down bolts and lightnings from heaven they could not hurt us or do us any harm if we were such men as we ought to be; for if man were truly as he ought to be, every evil, every tribulation, would be turned into blessings; for we know what said the Apostle, that all things work together for good to them that love God."

—FATHER G. JOSEPH GUSTAFSON, S.S.

July 1

Bless the Lord, all winds, sing praise to him and highly exalt him for ever. —Daniel 3:43

JULY'S warm days sometime give way to a little cool weather, a gentle change of pace in nature's routine. And while we bask in sunshine the other half of our hemisphere faces winter.

IN A WAY life resembles these opposing weather patterns. Happiness is often touched by sadness; sorrows are seldom totally unrelieved by joy. Likewise while some people are happy others are sad. The seasons steadily change from one to the other and the effects of one influence the other; April showers brighten the May flowers.

IN LIFE, maturity lies in balancing joys and sorrows, in recognizing the proportioned design of God which affects our lives as much as our weather. Warmth which pleases a Panamanian may be uncomfortable for us just as cold to an Eskimo is freezing to us. So too pains and pleasures are given to us purposefully and proportionally by God.

—FATHER JAMES A. CLARK

July 2

"Here rests in honored glory an American soldier known but to God." —Tomb of the Unknowns

THE ceremonial at the Tomb of the Unknowns is very impressive. It goes on hour by hour without any let-up, no matter what the season or the weather. And the "rubrics" are minute. They must be carried out with military perfection; and the crowds of visitors look on in meditative silence. This constant vigil is kept for "symbolic" soldiers — known only to God — who shed their blood that we might live.

BUT THE ONE who shed His Blood that we might live forever is not unknown, except to those who do not care, or to those who have not as yet heard the "good news" of salvation.

WE CALL the Blood of Jesus His "Most Precious Blood" because it poured out of the veins of God Himself as a sign of God's love for us. In that Blood was pardon and grace and love and holiness and peace. In the blessed Eucharist each day, that Blood cries out from earth to heaven; it flows from Him to us and brings us life forever.

—FATHER JOHN C. SELNER, S.S.

July 3

. . . Whatever you do, do all to the glory of God.
—I Corinthians 10:31

ONE of the very great priests of our time was the late Jesuit Father Daniel Lord. One of his friends aspired to the very strict Trappist order. He sought the advice of Father Lord. This is what he told him.

HENCEFORTH your life is God and yourself. Stay close to God and let Him do the worrying about you.

Your life will be hard. Offer that up for sinners.

Offer up some of your work for priests.

Keep your prayers simple.

Make your spiritual reading largely the Gospels. Read them over slowly and thoughtfully.

Try to do any job, important or trivial, with pride in it and wholeheartedly.

Watch your disposition. Keep your mind cheerful, at peace and content.

Never decline any joy you are asked to do if it is at all possible.

Make your answer to commands, requests, a simple, "Yes, Lord."

Remember that grace is the smile in your soul. Keep smiling!

Grow! When you stop growing spiritually, you are dead.
—FATHER ALBERT A. MURRAY, C.S.P.

July 4

This God is my strong refuge, and has made my way safe.
—2 Samuel 22:33

AS we celebrate our nation's birthday, we praise God for the many blessings He has showered upon our country. At this time we reflect upon our humble beginnings, and we should also pause to re-examine our national purposes and goals. Our motto says "In God We Trust." Yet, our Supreme Court forbids the use of God's name in the classroom. The Supreme Court also allowed abortion to become legalized.

GOD WAS not pushed into the background when our forefathers founded this country. He was placed right in the middle of the political arena. Let us pray to God for our country and its leaders today, asking Him to enlighten and guide them.
—MARGARET H. MALSAM

July 5

O Lord, by these things men live, and in all these is the life of my spirit. Oh, restore me to health and make me live! —Isaiah 38:16

S T. ANTHONY (1502-1539) was always mindful of the Lord's presence and of His injunctions. Seeing the needs of the poor for medical treatment, he studied medicine at the famous University of Padua. But after starting practice as a doctor he decided that he must learn to cure souls as well as bodies, for the two are inseparable. So he studied theology, which enabled him not only to comfort the sick but also to teach Christian doctrine to young and old.

AFTER HIS ORDINATION in Milan in 1530, he encouraged some holy women to found a congregation called the Angelicals to rescue girls fallen into evil ways. Then with four fellow priests he formed the Clerks Regular of St. Paul, or Barnabites, approved by Pope Clement VII to promote public preaching, even on street corners, and faithful ministering of the sacraments in Milan's many churches. By these works St. Anthony blunted the attacks Luther was then making against the Church. He was canonized by Pope Leo XIII in 1897.

—PAUL H. KOCHER

July 6

Let no one despise your youth, but set the believers an example in speech and conduct, in love, in faith, in purity. —I Timothy 4:12

S T. MARIA GORETTI was born less than a century ago and was buried, a twelve-year-old martyr, in 1902. Her murderer lived to attend her canonization in the Holy Year of 1950.

WHY DID she die so violent a death? She resisted rape, convinced that she should give her undefiled body to God rather than give in to any human considerations. That is wisdom and devotion far beyond her twelve earthly years. But it was a heavenly wisdom that she learned from her earliest years.

AND WHAT A LESSON it teaches us! In our permissive society, when God's gift of sex is made common and even a source of humor, St. Maria Goretti tells us to treasure this power that God has created. In sex, we share the power of the creating God. By self control, we tell Him thanks. The sacrifice of celibacy bears witness to this great power.

—FATHER CHARLES DOLLEN

July 7

Awake, you drunkards, and weep. . . . —Joel 1:5

HABITS save energy. Whether good or bad, habits are nature's way of avoiding effort. A person does a certain thing time and time again. Soon, there's no other way to do it. So when some people feel down and out, or lonesome, or just plain bored, they get the bottle. Before they realize it, the bottle has become their way to solve moodiness or grippiness. It takes only a short while until they are problem drinkers, if not alcoholics.

HABITS of whining, of vicious gossip, or temper outbursts work the same way. Folks grow accustomed to answer their moods by these outlets. Personality is the sum of these habits, good or bad.

HABITUAL kindness, habitual prayerfulness, honesty, purity, sobriety, good will . . . all likewise grow by practice. Once learned and acquired, these "good" habits also save energy and become part of our way of life.

—FATHER ROBERT L. WILKEN

July 8

". . . One field would be rained upon, and the field on which it did not rain withered . . ." says the Lord. —Amos 4:7

ON a summer day, rain can be a most unwelcome visitor. But the moisture that dampens our picnic plans can mean salvation to a farmer. In the winter, snow means shovels and backaches for householders, a wonderful week-end for skiers.

LIFE is better viewed when we can see all sides of it. An architect sees a building as a thing of beauty; the mason knows it as a pile of stone. If we take a comprehensive view of life, we see each day as a step toward eternal happiness or damnation. Frustrations, irritations, shrink to their proper proportion.

TOMORROW it will rain. A preoccupied man will step on my foot. The car will leak oil. Should I get excited? Not if I am busy about saving my soul for eternity. Only an idler has time to be a fuss-budget. — Jesus, may I always ask, what is this in comparison with eternity? We get so much for so little.

—FATHER LEO J. TRESE

July 9

You have fixed all the bounds of the earth; you have made summer and winter. —Psalms 74:17

SUMMERTIME gives many opportunities for recreational activities. What do we do for entertainment, and where do we enjoy it? How many of us spend recreation with the idea and purpose of serving God thereby? Yet that is the ultimate motive that should determine all that we do and the places we go.

IF WE are not serving God through our recreation, we do not understand its real meaning. We are making "Wreckreation" spelled with a capital W out of our free time. Time is precious but the amount of time that God gives us is not as important as how we spend it. Everyone needs time off from the grind of daily routine but no one needs time off from God.

RECREATION ought to re-create us so that we study better, pray better, work better and think better.

—MSGR. HARRY J. WELP

July 10

Blessed is he whose transgression is forgiven. . . . —Psalms 32:1

THE contrite heart will bring God's Presence into being within our souls. This is the solution for removing the decayed sins and replacing them with a new humble beginning — a spiritual beginning. Having true sorrow for our past sins does wonders for our spiritual union with the Father. This new desire to walk the path of Christ is healthful and rewarding.

OUR FUTURE becomes brighter and new hope is developed as we plan to make a better life for our families, friends and ourselves. This is part of the converting process we are forming by listening to the small voice within.

BREAKING with our past becomes easier when we find this new type of hope in the Christ way. Our attitude toward others becomes a real and understanding love. Father, help us to listen to the small voice within.

—JOHN JULIUS FISHER

July 11

"The radiant crown of glory, with which the most pure brow of the Virgin Mother was encircled by God, seems to Us to shine more brilliantly." —Pope Pius XII

MARY OF NAZARETH never knew moral evil. But what is most touching about the sinlessness of Mary is her mother's compassion for the soiled, sad human being who is steeped in sin. *Holy Virgin of Virgins,* we cry to our Lady in her Litany, *Mother Most Pure, Mother Most Chaste, Mother Inviolate, Mother Undefiled, Mirror of Justice, Tower of Ivory, House of Gold;* and then: *Refuge of Sinners.*

IT IS A STRANGE THING, Christian man and woman, that the immaculate Mother of God should have a care for you or me. But she has. In all our misery she pities and loves us, like the true, good Mother that she is. And she will not give over until, in every sense, she has brought us to her Son.

THUS WE PRAY in one of the best-loved Marian prayers: *And after this our exile show unto us the blessed fruit of thy womb.*
—FATHER VINCENT P. MCCORRY, S.J.

July 12

". . . From this time forth I make you hear new things. . . ."
—Isaiah 48:6

THE Christian whose heart is open to his neighbor will know well what it means to be a good listener. But on the whole, listening isn't the easiest virtue to cultivate. We seem to be a people much more taken up with hearing ourselves or having others hear us talk. A worthwhile experiment might be to think back after a conversation, and try to remember what we have said. Chances are we'll remember many more of our own comments than those of others.

EXAMINING how well we listen to others might be a good indicator of how well we listen to God. Often when we pray, we feel that we must always be the ones to speak; and when we run out of words, the prayer is over.

IT MAY BE good to remember that each of our prayers should first begin with an acknowledgment of the Lordship of God. After that admission has been made, our minds should be set in the context of listening to what Our Lord may have to say to us.
—JAMES M. SULLIVAN, M.M.

July 13

Fathers, do not provoke your children to anger, but bring them up in the discipline and instruction of the Lord. —Ephesians 6:4

THE parent who has to persuade with power and punches is a frightening example of a puny personality. The bully parent can instill fear for awhile but then the children grow up and they fear no longer. They simply hate.

THE GENTLE parent — the gentleman and lady — can discipline for a lifetime with a tender love that breeds respect. No one likes a bully and if parents expect respect they must unfold the fist into a gentle hand again.

VARIOUS are the causes for parental violence: uncontrollable anger, inability to cope with a crisis, inferiority complex or simply the mistaken notion that "pounding out a kid" is the best way to teach him a lesson. Whatever the cause, the effect is always disgusting and parents should seek professional help to control their violent emotions. Remember: "Nothing is so strong as gentleness."
—FATHER JOHN C. TORMEY

July 14

He who closes his ear to the cry of the poor will himself cry out and not be heard. —Proverbs 21:13

IF there is an American heresy, it is that of "mind your own business." A person can have a minimum of concern for others and the rest of the community will not disapprove. "Let each one care for himself" is the motto.

CHRIST'S LIFE and teaching was a direct refutation of this philosophy. "Whoever says he loves God, and loves not his neighbor, is a liar." Knowing this, how can we become infected with such an attitude?

THERE ARE natural deterrents to helping others. We fear being over-enthusiastic or injudicious in our efforts to help. We want to avoid becoming unduly involved. Most of all, we may lack practice. It takes a practiced eye to see where help is needed. If we look only for material need, we may not see a need for counseling, or sympathy, or love.
—FATHER LEO J. TRESE

July 15

Discretion will watch over you: understanding will guard you.
—Proverbs 2:11

THE man who invented the pencil really did us a great service. However, he did us an even greater service in using his foresight to attach an eraser, for in doing so, he showed he understood human nature. With the eraser, we can write something, err — erase the mistake — and continue.

IN LIFE, we should allow one another the same privilege, that is, the privilege of failure. Too often we expect others to be perfect and right on all occasions and in all circumstances. In doing so, we are really denying them the fact that they are human. The person who never made a mistake in life never did *anything*.

"BE YE perfect as your Heavenly Father is perfect" is a goal, not a state we're born to. In reaching toward it, we have our setbacks, pitfalls, and failures. But don't stop there! It's not the mistake that's so bad, it's the failure to erase it.
—FATHER NICHOLAS P. SMITH

July 16

Then I will go to the altar of God, to God my exceeding joy.
—Psalms 43:4

AT Mass, following the prayer over the gifts, fitting the season's theme, the priest enjoins us to "Lift up your hearts."

ONE CAN feel an almost physical raising of one's heart to God. Negatively, do we not often speak of being downhearted, of broken hearts, of heartache? To anyone who has experienced these feelings, the terms are quite accurate. In just what lies the connection between states of mind and bodily reactions, is not clearly known. But not solely for poetic reasons, one does not write to a faraway love, "My knee aches for you," but because the emotion is specifically felt in the area of the heart.

THEREFORE, when we lift up our hearts to God — as children raise their faces to catch raindrops or snowflakes on their tongues — as beggars hold out their caps — as, at celebrations, people hold out their mugs for drink — we may feel an actual lightening of the load. "It is right and just to give Him praise."
—ANONYMOUS

July 17

"Come, let us return and visit the brethren in every city where we proclaimed the word of the Lord, and see how they are."
—Acts 15:36

THE old Spanish Missions of California are not really that old, if we compare their age to the missions of Latin America and Canada. By the standards of Mexico, Peru, Montreal and Quebec they are rather young.

YET the string of missions that dots the coast of the State of California bears eloquent witness to the burning missionary zeal of Friar Junipero Serra and his team of Franciscans. From San Diego in the south to the northernmost regions of the San Francisco Bay area they dot the landscape like the Litany of the Saints.

THE PROTOMARTYR of the Missions, Fra Luis Jayme lies buried near Mission San Diego de Alcala. During an Indian uprising he was bludgeoned to death, with his familiar cry on his lips: *Amar a Dios, hijos!* "Love God, my children!"

—FATHER CHARLES DOLLEN

July 18

You shall not take vengeance or bear any grudge against the sons of your own people, but you shall love your neighbor as yourself.
—Leviticus 19:18

TO seek peace and contentment is a natural longing on our part to feel and be part of the grace sent by the Father. Our spiritual self is longing to blossom out. Unless we include our neighbors in our spiritual plans, we cannot grow into the realization of peace and contentment. We must have the Christ love for neighbors, to find the love we seek.

THE ROAD to peace and contentment is a long and narrow road; many that seek and find this road, eventually fall by the wayside. Why? Some lose faith, some lose direction, and some just give up due to the obstacles put in their way.

CHRIST is always ready to guide the honest seeker; the road seems to widen with the realization of Christ's Presence. Father, we seek peace and contentment, give us faith, direction and perseverance.

—JOHN JULIUS FISHER

July 19

"Woe to us! For nothing like this has happened before. . . ."
—I Samuel 4:7

IT'S very sad to be around people whose feelings are easily hurt. When a person barks his shins, or stubs his toe, he cries out to high heaven but a person never becomes vocal when feelings are hurt. In fact, there is a peculiar kind of silence — a clamming-up.

A PERSON whose feelings have been hurt draws back into a shell and seems very cold and unresponsive. He will speak only when spoken to. It is obvious that something has happened but it is best not to approach the person and ask: "Anything wrong?" This is just what he has been waiting for, for there is a certain pleasure in having hurt feelings.

HURT FEELINGS get well of their own accord, if questions are not asked and the person is permitted to suffer in silence. The milk of human kindness sours quickly around hurt feelings. Hurt feelings suffer quick relapses if the victim can make everyone uncomfortable.

—FATHER ALBERT A. MURRAY, C.S.P.

July 20

Let us consider how to stir up one another to love and good works. . . . —Hebrews 10:24

PERSONAL works of mercy among sick, the poor, orphans and the illiterate seem to mark each saint whose birthday we celebrate this week. Today a saint's love for the needy and the slum dwellers must also find channels for changing basic defects in our way of life. The system and the structure cannot be allowed to grind out injustice, anymore than we Christians can allow an individual to go hungry or homeless.

SOCIAL JUSTICE and reform of our social structure does not wear the appealing halo of a St. Jerome carrying a plague victim on his back, or personally nursing a distraught mental patient. To most, social and legal reform sounds too much like politics. But who said saints can't be wise politicians?

CHRIST will smile even more warmly today upon the groups of Christians who work to root out racial discrimination, scandalous housing, subhuman standards of living at home and abroad.

—FATHER ROBERT L. WILKEN

July 21

"You shall love your neighbor as yourself." —Mark 12:31

WE love our friends and relatives. But Christ said there is no merit in just loving your friends. "My command is to love your enemies, pray for your persecutors."

HOW CAN we love those who annoy us? Strangely when we began to pray in earnest for them, we began to see why these people act as they do. Soon we began to sympathize more with them, and the walls between us begin to crumble.

LET US remember not to judge others, but give others the benefit of a doubt. "Let me not criticize my brother until I have walked a mile in his moccasins," goes an old Indian saying. Could it be that the reason why we take pleasure in criticizing others so much is the fact that we feel inadequate and need to build ourselves up? By pointing out faults of others, which we may not have, we make ourselves feel superior. But we have many other faults that are perhaps hidden from our own eyes. Christ said let Him throw the first rock that is without any sin.

—MARGARET H. MALSAM

July 22

He who walks in integrity walks securely, but he who perverts his ways will be found out. —Proverbs 10:9

A DAILY good life involves these four steps: think — pray — resolve — act.

THINK — Where did I come from? Where am I going? How am I going to get there? My faith answers all these questions.

PRAY — Every day I must pray for the help, the grace that I need in my particular state of life.

RESOLVE — Am I expecting everything from God and doing nothing in return? I must do better by getting rid of my biggest fault.

ACT — Thought and prayer produce resolution, but resolution is dead without action.

I MUST fight my faults with definite action and not vague resolution. I must keep trying, no matter how many times I fail. God will not help me if I do not want to be helped.

—MSGR. HARRY J. WELP

July 23

"Lord, when did we see thee hungry and feed thee, or thirsty and give thee drink?" —Matthew 25:37

I WAS thirsty and you gave Me a drink. When? When I came disguised in the plumber, the delivery man, the newspaper boy, the garbage collector — that hot day. You offered Me a cool drink. On that cold day you gave Me a cup of steaming hot coffee.

EVERY DAY you prepared and often poured the tea, the coffee, the milk into the cups of your family circle — several times a day. I was there in them. I drank.

YOU PAID for my cup of coffee during the coffee break. You treated Me to a Coke. You gave Me a drink!

THOUGHTFULLY you put Cokes into the cooler for the teen-agers who spent an evening in the basement planning activities. I was there. I was thirsty in the least of My brethren, and you gave Me a drink.

—THERESITA POLZIN

July 24

He has made everything beautiful in its time. —Ecclesiastes 3:11

SUMMER words are pleasant words. *Holidays,* sunshine (few fail to welcome the warming shafts of the sun), *picnics, ponds, crickets,* and dozens more speak to us of joy. Summer means vacations, a change from our regular routine of work or study, an opportunity to refresh ourselves, a chance to catch our breath before commencing again with the duties of days that slowly dissolve into years. Summer words bespeak quiet and calm, friends and friendship, freedom and fun. Summer marks the season of tranquillity. If we sense these sentiments in our souls we will reflect contentment and calm in our countenance.

WORDS CONVEY love or hate; intelligence or ignorance; they hurt or heal; condemn or condone. Aside from our relationships with loved ones, words are about the only means of contact that we have with others.

EXAMINE your conversation to discover whether you use *summer* or somber words. Act accordingly.

—FATHER JAMES A. CLARK

July 25

"To you has been given the secret of the kingdom of God."

—Mark 4:11

THE Apostle, St. James the Great, was a special friend of Jesus, with John and Peter. He was present on Mount Tabor and saw Jesus glorified. He was in the Garden of Olives when Jesus poured forth His bloody sweat for the sins of the world.

THE SHRINE of St. James at Compostella, Spain was one of the most famous in the world, ranking with Rome and Jerusalem. His relics were taken there, probably for fear of the Arabs in Jerusalem.

LITTLE is known of the life of St. James. But the most important detail is not lacking: his nearness to Christ. So too with us. Our lives are not to be measured by our activities and our accomplishments, not the position we have or the job we hold. There is one norm only — our nearness to God measured in terms of love. Ask yourself the question: How close to God am I? Answer it truthfully.

—FATHER TITUS CRANNY, S.A.

July 26

"Honor your father and your mother, that your days may be long in the land which the Lord your God gives you." —Exodus 20:12

THE Mother of the Blessed Virgin Mary and her spouse, Joachim, were childless for many years. When they had given up all hope God sent them Mary who was destined to be the Mother of God. Anne and Joachim consecrated Mary to God and gave her back to Him. Their example is one to be imitated by all parents who do not encourage, who even hinder, the boy or girl who wants to enter the priesthood or religious life.

ST. ANNE should be the patroness of all mothers of Priests, Sisters and Brothers. She should be the model for parents who find in their child an inclination toward serving God in the priesthood or religious. Parents should pray to her that one of their own will be blessed with a call from God.

CHRIST NEEDS more of our young people to give themselves to His Church in the work for souls.

—MSGR. HARRY J. WELP

July 27

Thy testimonies are my heritage for ever; yea, they are the joy of my heart. —Psalms 119:111

OUR Lady is the Queen and Mother of contemplatives. Not only was Mary closer to Our Lord than anyone else; we are also distinctly told that she reflected deeply — meditated, that is — on what He said and did. Thus we read in St. Luke's second chapter, *but Mary treasured up all these sayings, and reflected on them in her heart.* Again, *The father and mother of the Child were still wondering over all that was said of Him.* Yet again, *His mother kept in her heart the memory of all this.*

VIRGIN MOST REFLECTIVE, Virgin most prayerful, Virgin most contemplative: these are meaningful titles which might justly be included in a private litany to our Lady. Surely this good Mother, whose contemplation of the Light of the World was so deep and uninterrupted, will eagerly assist us in our honest efforts to practice a prayer that will be far more than the repetition of pious formulas.
—FATHER VINCENT P. McCORRY, S.J.

July 28

Let your light so shine before men, that they may see your good works and give glory to your Father who is in heaven. —Matthew 5:16

THE Beatitudes are a continual challenge to many of the values we so easily take for granted. They mean that wealth and status are not in themselves worth pouring out our life to obtain. The beatitudes also mean that self-assertion and strife for our own gain at the expense of others' needs is not a Christian way of living.

IF WE reflect quietly upon the beatitudes, we begin to see where they relate to our own life. A number of them refer directly to the way we relate to others: "blessed are the gentle . . .," "blessed are the merciful . . .," "blessed are the peacemakers. . . ." These beatitudes relate to what Our Lord also says about not being the source of quarrels and bitterness.

OUR LORD was very clear for example on the need to control and overcome anger. If we give way to anger and resentment, as will undoubtedly happen from time to time, then the sacred duty of reconciliation arises.
—JAMES MICHAEL SULLIVAN

July 29

Do you not know that in a race all the runners compete, but only one receives the prize? So run that you may obtain it.
— I Corinthians 9:24

T HE late Vince Lombardi, the famous coach of the Green Bay Packers, once said, "Fatigue makes a coward of a player. Any man — any team — that gives in to it, will never be a winner."

AS IN football, so in life. It, too is a game in which we all participate. We strive for the ultimate goal which is union with God in eternity. St. Paul describes it to the Corinthians this way, "The athlete's prize is perishable. The one we seek is imperishable."

THE GAME of life has its downs and fumbles, its good times and bad, for all of us. There are occasions when we feel like throwing in the towel, sitting back and not lifting a finger to help our cause. We're tired! We're fed up! But it is in these moments of fatigue, of weakness, of temptation, that we must fight on. These are the moments in life that make us winners, or losers.

WE CANNOT afford to quit or give in, because in this game of life the *only* way to fail is to give up trying.

—FATHER NICHOLAS P. SMITH

July 30

. . . Grow in the grace and knowledge of our Lord and Savior Jesus Christ. —2 Peter 3:18

W HY do things the hard way? For instance, we know we need the inspiration that comes from spiritual reading. Do we immediately classify as spiritual only those books which are profound enough to make us work hard at reading them? A treatise on mysticism is fine, if we have progressed enough spiritually to understand and appreciate it, but the value does not depend on its difficulty.

WE DON'T HAVE to suffer in order to benefit from spiritual reading. Reading we enjoy is fine (even a Catholic magazine, or a good Catholic novel) as long as it supplies us with thoughts about God, and our relationship with Him. The rest is up to the Holy Spirit. He will pick out the one or two thoughts He knows we can use, and He will give us the grace to understand and remember. If we enjoy it, we are less likely to put it off indefinitely.

—FATHER LEO J. TRESE

The Lord your God is in your midst, a warrior who gives victory. —Zephaniah 3:17

S T. Ignatius of Loyola (1491-1556), son of a noble Spanish family, was in his youth a soldier of Spain until wounds disabled him and he became, after 1521, a soldier of God. This happened while he lay bedridden. His only books were a Life of Jesus and a volume about the lives of the Saints. Upon studying these he dedicated himself to Mary, and at her shrine in Montserrat hung up his rapier and dagger.

OUT OF HIS SUFFERINGS he distilled a book, *Spiritual Exercises,* which set forth a series of prayers and disciplines for the attainment of holiness. This later became the handbook of all who aspired to join his Order, the Society of Jesus (Jesuits). Since he had been educated in several Spanish universities, those attracted to him were likewise men of high education. In this way his Society became the intellectual leaders of the Church, especially against the Protestants.

MANY Jesuits won crowns of martyrdom by the headsman's axe. Ignatius himself was canonized by Pope Gregory XV in 1622.
—PAUL H. KOCHER

August 1

My steps have held fast to thy paths, my feet have not slipped.
—Psalms 17:5

S T. ALPHONSUS was a great theologian and theologians deal in what is morally right and wrong. Our unconscious acts such as the internal workings of our body and those idle gestures we may make while we are speaking, have no morality. When we are conscious, however, all of the actions we perform as rational beings have a morality and that is why spiritual writers tell us there is no standing still in the moral plane. We are either becoming better or becoming worse because our conscious actions are either good or bad.

SOME THINGS like walking or talking are indifferent in themselves but when we do them consciously they are always done for a purpose and they become good or bad, according to that purpose. So if we are walking in order to commit murder, the walking becomes bad. On the other hand if we are walking in order to take care of the sick, the walking is good.
—MSGR. JOSEPH B. LUX

August 2

Man of God . . . aim at righteousness, godliness, faith, love, steadfastness, gentleness. —I Timothy 6:11

T HE place to take the true measure of a man is not the forum or the field . . . but at his own fireside. There he lays aside his mask, and you may judge whether he is demon or angel, king or cur, hero or humbug.

I CARE not what the world says of him. If his children rush to the door to greet him, and love's own sunshine illuminates the face of his wife when she hears his foot fall, you may take it for granted he is true gold, for his home's a heaven, and the humbug never gets that near the great white throne of God. *(Way of St. Francis)*

CHARITY, says the proverb, begins at home. And charity, says the dictionary, is loving-kindness. Our own family has the first right to our politeness, our generosity, our considerateness. They say no man is a hero to his valet. The latter observes too much. But how many heroes have valets? The man who is looked up to in his own home is hero aplenty! It should not be hard being kind to those we love most of all.
—FATHER JOSEPH E. MANTON, C.SS.R.

August 3

The grace of God has appeared for the salvation of all men, training us to renounce irreligion and worldly passions, and to live sober, upright, and godly lives in this world. . . . —Titus 2:11

NO matter who you are, you should be an apostle. If you take your religion seriously, you will desire to be something for Christ. His love will urge you. Every day the world grows larger and more open, and there are more souls to be saved or brought nearer to God. Never before in the history of the human race has the Christian who would be an apostle had such an opportunity as now.

SOMETIMES you will ask: "What can I do alone?" The history of the Church is the answer. It is not numbers but willingness; not learning but self-sacrifice; not even any special skill or training, but a strong desire to do good, a strong hand to put to the plow. That not mere numbers make the difference, the past has clearly shown. Newman says well: "Moses was one, Elias was one, David was one, Leo was one, Athanasius was one. Grace ever works by the few. It is the keen vision, the intense conviction, the indomitable resolve of the few. It is the blood of the martyr, it is the prayer of the saint, it is the heroic deed, it is the momentary crisis, it is the concentrated energy of a look or a word which is the instrument of heaven."

—ARCHBISHOP RICHARD J. CUSHING

August 4

". . . He who is least among you all is the one who is great."
—Luke 9:48

ST. JOHN VIANNEY is a good example of how God picks the least-likely-to-succeed, humanly speaking, to become the most successful in doing what He wants done for the salvation of people. In the judgment of one bishop, John was not fit for the priesthood because his marks were poor. Another bishop rated him differently and ordained him to a priesthood of wonderful service and redemptive effect in a small town in France that was as unlikely a place as John was a person for greatness.

WE CAN'T begin to imagine what good God can do with us and through us, if we just let Him have His way.

JOHN VIANNEY let it happen. He became the Curé of Ars, a confessor sought by thousands of people for spiritual direction and a pastor of such merit that he has been proclaimed the patron of parish priests.

—FATHER FELICIAN A. FOY, O.F.M.

August 5

"My soul magnifies the Lord, and my spirit rejoices in God my Savior."
—Luke 1:46-47

M ARY is so kind and courteous that she is ever with us; keeps us company in solitude; accompanies us on our journeys; counsels us in doubt; consoles us in affliction; assists us in sickness; defends us from our enemies, visible and invisible; encourages us in fear; and protects us from the anger and vengeance of God.

IF WE CALL her, she answers promptly; if we salute her, she courteously returns the salutation; if we praise her, she kindly thanks us; if we do her any service, she abundantly reimburses us; if we show her faith and love, she gives us the most tender proofs of her affection.

SAINT Catherine of Siena said, Mary is a most sweet bait that God has prepared to catch the hearts of men.
—FATHER SEBASTIAN V. RAMGE, O.C.D.

August 6

. . . A bright cloud overshadowed them, and a voice from the cloud said, "This is my beloved Son, with whom I am well pleased; listen to him." —Matthew 17:5

T HE Feast of the Transfiguration celebrates the revelation of Christ's Divinity to Peter, James and John.

CHRIST must be the center of our life. But we must believe that Christ was True God and True Man; it is essential to our faith. Today the Divinity of Christ is under attack in some theological circles. That's the problem of the theologians who would diminish Him. Don't let it become your problem, believe in Him as True God and True Man.

SOME PEOPLE say that Jesus was such a good man that even if you don't believe in His Divinity that's all right, you can keep Him as the model of a good man. But good men don't lie and Our Lord said "He was truly the Son of God, that He and the Father are One." Believe Him, for this is an essential of our belief that cannot be placed aside.

—DALE FRANCIS

August 7

Hear a just cause, O Lord; attend to my cry! Give ear to my prayer.
—Psalms 17:1

PRAYER, however we may look at it, is simply conversation with God.

YET THIS noisy, rushing world in which we live sweeps us along without time to stop and talk with the One who knows us best, knows our problems better than we do, and is always ready to give us a hearing.

WE DO NOT pause to think nor pause to speak to Him, and so we are almost strangers. We are embarrassed when we are left alone with our thoughts before God, almost as though we are left alone with a total stranger with whom we have nothing in common to talk about. Even though we may have addressed Him in our prayers many times a day — in the Mass, with our breviary, with our prayerbooks — but always in formalized prayers, neatly composed and printed. The words of someone else, not our own; seldom a spontaneous and candid conversation with the One we have every reason to love and trust and speak to without fear of betrayal or lack of complete understanding.

—BISHOP THOMAS K. GORMAN, Dallas-Fort Worth, Texas

August 8

"The Spirit of the Lord is upon me, because he has anointed me to preach good news to the poor. He has sent me to proclaim release to the captives . . . to set at liberty those who are oppressed."
—Luke 4:18

ST. DOMINIC is honored among many other things not only for the religious organization he founded, the Order of Preachers, but for his notable part in the preservation and spread of the Faith at a time it was greatly jeopardized. A particularly repulsive rival religion, the Albigensians, had overrun great areas of Europe, threatening both Church and state. Against them Dominic set his first forces which soon grew into a strong right arm of the Church in the Thirteenth Century.

SIGNIFICANT to us is Dominic's insistence on the priority of self-sanctification and the spread of the Gospel after the fashion of the Apostles. "We must sow the seed, not hoard it," he said as he dispersed his disciples to every part of Europe.

—FATHER G. JOSEPH GUSTAFSON, S.S.

August 9

God said, "Let us make man in our image, after our likeness; and let them have dominion over the fish of the sea, and over the birds of the air, and over the cattle . . . and over every creeping thing that creeps upon the earth." —Genesis 1:26

WHEN you see a small animal, your first reaction is to cuddle and protect it from harm. Yet the Scripture tells us that God gave man dominion over the animals.

IF YOU HAVE SUCH a tender care for something over which you have control, God's tenderness toward His creation is at least as great as yours. That is why we must always have confidence in our heavenly Father. He is ever gracious and helpful.

WHEN A SMALL ANIMAL is hungry or hurt, it cannot receive help from man unless it goes to a human being. In the same way, we must go to our heavenly Father when we need His help.

ONE OF THE REAL JOYS of helping animals is the warmth they return when they show their gratitude. The wag of a puppy's tail makes us glad for whatever small effort we took. Do you always thank God for the times He has helped you? It does not take any grand gesture on your part; just a smile, a whispered thank you.

—FATHER DONALD F. X. CONNOLLY

August 10

Turn my eyes from looking at vanities; and give me life in thy ways. —Psalms 119:37

HOW often Brother Lawrence is mentioned in spiritual books. A 17th century lay Carmelite Brother, he practiced "The Presence of God."

ASSIGNED to culinary duty, Brother Lawrence wrote: "The time of action is not different from that of prayer. I enjoy God with as great tranquillity in the hurry of my kitchen where frequently many people call upon me at the same time for different things, as if I was on my knees at the holy sacrament. Nor is it any ways necessary to be concerned with great matters. . . . I put my little egg-cake into the frying pan for the love of God."

LIFE IS so daily. We can identify with Brother Lawrence who advised: "If the vessel of our soul is still tossed with winds and storms let us wake the Lord, who reposes in it, and He will calm the sea."

—MARION EGAN

August 11

The maiden was very fair to look upon, a virgin, whom no man had known. —Genesis 24:16

SAINT CLARE is likened to the "wise virgin, whom the Lord found watching."

UNLIKE her beloved friend and spiritual father, St. Francis, St. Clare lived a life completely hidden from the world. In her cloistered convent where she founded the Poor Clares in Assisi, she loved and suffered and died. God has shown her to the world by miracles and the great devotion of the pilgrims to her tomb.

LIKE ALL cloistered religious, St. Clare can help us to see that at the end of life only holiness and love really matter. In utter poverty, she was rich in joy and peace. In silence, she sang to her God. In death, she found life. Let us ask St. Clare to help us see money and material things at their true value, and to use them only to help ourselves and our fellowmen to eternal life.

—SISTER M. CHARLES BORROMEO, C.S.C.

August 12

"Fear not, little flock, for it is your Father's good pleasure to give you the kingdom. . . ." —Luke 12:32

THE fear of God which is the beginning of wisdom means respect for Him and His judgments. It does not mean dread of God as a tyrant. Yet, some people have exaggerated ideas of what this fear is and means. It might be good for them to remember: God wills good for all men and knows, as a loving Father, how to give good things to those who love Him.

GOD BRINGS good from evil in the total working out of His plan for salvation, in time and eternity. And the sufferings of this life are not to be compared with the good prepared in heaven for those who love Him.

GOD DOES NOT punish us for the sins of others, even though we may undergo suffering as a result of the evil they do. God pardons the sins of those who seek His forgiveness with true sorrow and submission to His will.

GOD SO LOVES us that He gave His Son over to death that we might have life in Him.

—FATHER FELICIAN A. FOY, O.F.M.

August 13

Their voice goes out through all the earth. . . .   —Psalms 19:4

MAN has developed countless ways to communicate his ideas and feelings to other men but simple spoken words continue to be among his most perfect expressions.

WORDS of encouragement, kindness, sympathy, thanks and love, when expressed as honestly as possible usually hit their mark even though they be faltering, clumsy and nervous. Every man wants to communicate deeply with others and most of his attempts are recognized as sincere and meaningful.

NEVERTHELESS there are points in life where the spoken word cannot express what we mean. When we experience exuberant joy, crushing depression, deep mutual love or loneliness, we want to laugh, to cry, to hold and to be held. In short, we want to give a part of the core of ourselves where so often words are just noise. This is what God does.

—JULIO GIULIETTI, M.M.

August 14

". . . Even the darkness is not dark to thee, the night is bright as the day; for darkness is as light with thee."   —Psalms 139:12

DID you ever look at stained-glass windows, while, standing on the outside of a church? They look dull and uninteresting. You see leaded glass, criss-crossed. But wait! Step inside. You'll find a beautiful transformation. While the light streams through the same windows, you now see many biblical scenes each relating a beautiful story. The sun peeks through the windows and shines on the altar. Mellow shades of every conceivable color tint the environment.

OUTSIDE, it is different. So, too, with our heart. Faith must enlighten our minds. Without it, we are robbed of the greatest beauty and happiness. Let faith and love of God enter your heart and your soul becomes illuminated with a special kind of beauty even as the church windows take on life when the sun shines through them. When the night is black outside, and the church within is lighted, the colors of the windows stream out into the world. They welcome all to enter the house of God and partake of the glory.

LET the light of faith shine in your soul forever enriching your life and the life of others.

—MARIE LAYNE

August 15

A great portent appeared in heaven, a woman clothed with the sun, with the moon under her feet, and on her head a crown of twelve stars.
—Revelation 12:1

MARY'S ASSUMPTION has many meanings. For the American worker it comes along at a time when it's too hot to work and too late for vacation. For the schoolboy it's one of the impossible Latin words he always gets mixed up with the Ascension.

MARY'S ASSUMPTION, however, means much more than that. We call it her crowning feast, you know, because it is the logical result of her dignity as the Immaculate Virgin Mother of God. It has two distinct aspects. One considers her bodily assumption into Heaven. The other views her coronation in Heaven with all the pomp and circumstance that only Heaven can lavish and which we poor mortals can only imagine.

MARY'S ASSUMPTION has a much more personal meaning for us. It is both a reminder and a rebuke. It comes along in the middle of August each year to remind us of the age-old, fundamental Catholic truth of the existence of Heaven. It is a rebuke to a sex-crazy people who have lost the meaning and importance of Christian modesty.
—FATHER VINCENT A. YZERMANS

August 16

Do not say to your neighbor, "Go, and come again, tomorrow I will give it" — when you have it with you. —Proverbs 3:28

A NEIGHBOR is, by definition, someone who happens to be near to us. We have little or nothing to say about who our next neighbor is going to be, for he will be God-given, not self-chosen. For our friends we can select those who have similar interests and people with whom we feel "at home."

BUT A NEIGHBOR is not necessarily a friend at all. He may have nothing in common with us — neither race, nor religion, education, social background, intelligence, nor even language.

WHO will your next neighbor be? An attractive person? Someone whose background or bearing will offend you? A stranger who needs your help? You will not chose him. God will . . . and God will note how you treat him.
—FATHER FRANCIS R. MOESLEIN

August 17

*Love is patient and kind; love is not jealous or boastful; it is not
arrogant or rude. Love does not insist on its own way. . . .*
                                                    —1 Corinthians 13:4-5

T HE operative word in marital love is "giving." The great
    paradox of love is that it is only in giving that we receive. Two
people invest a large share of themselves without consideration of
cost or dividend — this is the risk of a trusting and enduring love.

WHEN ONE tries to get more than he gives then the marriage
will suffer a drainage of its resources and dry up.

IT IS like a bank account. If you take out more than you give in
then do not expect any interest or dividends. The very same principle
is applicable to marital interest. As long as two people do not tire of
"giving," they will be less likely to "give up."
                                                    —FATHER JOHN C. TORMEY

August 18

*"Blessed are the peacemakers, for they shall be called sons of
God."*   —Matthew 5:9

F EW ideals have caused so many wars as peace. The trouble is
    that it is only peace on our own terms that we want. Our Lady
of Fatima warned us to pray and do penance to escape the scourge of
war. Have you ever watched a group of children daringly getting
deeper into trouble and thought, "They're really asking for it"?

BUT ON the more personal level, where most of us live, are we
peacemakers? "A gentle answer turneth away wrath." Gentle
answers like — "I'm sorry. I did not mean to hurt you." — "Why are
you angry?" — "Can I help?" — "Yes, you probably are right." —
"I can't agree with you, but you don't have to agree with me either,
you know." — "I didn't know that habit of mine bugged you." —
"O.K. Let's try it your way."

GENTLE WORDS. "Thank you." "Congratulations." "I love
you."
                                                    —TERRY MARTIN

August 19

Beloved, it is a loyal thing you do when you render any service to the brethren, especially to strangers who have testified to your love before the church. —3 John 5

THE laity in the Church — In the face of the present crisis, the world is honeycombed with reformers. Individuals as well as organizations are endeavoring to bring about changes for the better. We are continually hearing of new laws or other reforms which propose to cure every ill of society. Yet things are going from bad to worse. Pope Leo XIII indicated the right direction when he said: "Society can be healed in no other way than by a return to Christian life and Christian institutions." Unless we build on Christ and His Gospel, we build on sand. Christ lives and works in His Church. From her and through her salvation must come. But how shall the Church lead mankind back from naturalism and sin to a spiritual and religious regeneration? The falling away from God and religion came about in the face of the Church and of human society.

COUNTLESS men and women are gradually coming to the realization of the power for good that is in them, and are exercising every means to exert it. Many a devout teacher instills solid moral principles into the plastic minds of her young charges, many a zealous nurse upholds the laws of nature's God, many a professional man and poor working man also create a spirit of charity.

—ARCHBISHOP RICHARD J. CUSHING

August 20

"My Father, if it be possible, let this cup pass from me; nevertheless, not as I will, but as thou wilt." —Matthew 26:39

"MAN proposes, but God disposes." If St. Bernard had his way, he would have remained an unknown, obscure monk, hidden from the world. God, however, had different designs. He thrust Bernard upon the world scene of the twelfth century. He made the humble monk of Clairvaux the leader of men and counselor of emperors and popes.

FOR YOU and for me, as for St. Bernard, holiness ultimately consists in doing God's Will. That Divine Providence will lead and direct us. We need not fear, we need not plot and scheme and make plans for the future. Another Saint, Thomas More, said it so well long ago: "Never trouble thy mind for anything that will come to thee in this world. Nothing will come but what God wills. . . ."

—FATHER VINCENT A. YZERMANS

August 21

On this rock I will build my church, and the powers of death shall not prevail against it. —Matthew 16:18

THIS visitor to St. Peter's in Rome was so overwhelmed by its majestic proportions that we tended to linger at the smaller altars, such as that of St. Pius X. Attired in papal robes, face and hands covered with golden masks, the Saint's body lies in a glass enclosure beneath the altar.

JOSEPH SARTO, an Italian, born in poverty in 1835, ascended to the papacy in 1903. Until his death in 1914 he continued to stress the importance of early and daily Communion.

HOW OFTEN he must have reflected on Christ's words to that first Vicar: "Simon, son of John, do you love me more than these?" Peter, to whom patience was not a native virtue, answered "Yes" three times, and received the same admonition three times from the Son of God: "Feed my sheep."

—MARION EGAN

August 22

. . . At your right hand stands the queen in gold. . . . —Psalms 45:9

THE theme of this observance of the Queenship of the Blessed Virgin Mary, is the same as that of the last mystery of the Rosary, the crowning of Mary as Queen of heaven and earth, of men and angels. The memorial was decreed by Pope Pius XII in 1954 near the close of a Marian Year marking the centenary of the proclamation of the dogma of the Immaculate Conception. The Pope urged:

"LET ALL strive vigilantly and strenuously to reproduce each according to his own condition, in their own souls and in their own conduct the exalted virtues of our heavenly Queen and our most loving Mother. And hence it will follow that those who are counted as Christians, honoring and imitating their Queen and Mother, will finally realize that they are truly brothers and, spurning jealousies and immoderate desires, may promote social charity, respect the rights of the weak, and love peace. And let no one consider himself a child of Mary to be taken readily under her most powerful protection unless, according to her example, he practices justice, meekness and chastity, and devotes himself to true brotherhood, not harming or hurting anyone, but rather helping and consoling."

—FATHER FELICIAN A. FOY, O.F.M.

August 23

The Lord your God will bless you in all your produce and in all the work of your hands, so that you will be altogether joyful.
—Deuteronomy 16:15

NOT all of us are pretty or handsome. But all of us are beautiful. Take a look at your hand. See the curves and contours which make up your fingers. Notice the different kinds of skin on the palm and the back of your hand. See the small holes and the cracks and crevices. Notice how you can flex every joint.

REALIZE that with these hands, you take care of most of your needs. Some people use their hands to play the violin; others use their hands to console the sick; the priest uses his hands to change bread and wine into the Body and Blood of Christ.

FEW INVENTIONS of mankind can approach the perfection of the human hand. And yet the hands are only a small part of your entire body. God lavished so many things on us that it is a shame if we let any slight disfigurement lead us into thinking that we are not beautiful.
—FATHER DONALD F.X. CONNOLLY

August 24

. . . You shall not turn aside from the verdict which they declare to you, either to the right hand or to the left. —Deuteronomy 17:11

ALL of the Apostles excepting St. John were martyrs to the cause of the Gospel of Christ. They were in contrast to the present-day attitude which excuses us from fulfilling the law of God if it would hurt us financially or endanger our lives.

THIS IS KNOWN as the argument from consequences wherein we don't conduct ourselves according to what is right and wrong in the eyes of God but consider only what is useful to us.

IF SAINT Bartholomew had felt that way he would not have faced the certainty of a horrible martyrdom by preaching the Gospel to hostile people. He felt that his life was worth very little in comparison to the souls he saved.
—MSGR. JOSEPH B. LUX

August 25

I sought the Lord, and he answered me, and delivered me from all my fears.   —Psalms 33:4

THE future belongs to believers and not to skeptics and doubters. The future belongs to those who love, not to those who hate.

ST. LOUIS, the King of France, believed in the essential goodness of man and spent the years of his reign trying to establish an atmosphere in which the goodness of his people could flourish. In all this great king did, never did personal ambition share, for his only motives were the glory of God and the good of his subjects. When he was urged to execute the son of Hugh de la Marche for following his father in rebellion against the crown, Louis refused: "A son cannot refuse to obey his father." For many generations afterward, whenever the people were dissatisfied with their rulers, they demanded that abuses be reformed and justice impartially administered as it was in the reign of St. Louis.

FOR THIS Louis has remained to the present times "beloved of God and men, whose memory is blessed."

—FATHER SEBASTIAN V. RAMGE, O.C.D.

August 26

Where there is no prophecy the people cast off restraint, but blessed is he who keeps the law.   —Proverbs 29:18

IT is really quite simple and today quite the fashion to blame all evils on economic problems or social conditions as if man were some kind of predetermined and preconditioned creature without free will to be manipulated like the elements in a laboratory or to be managed like animals. This is crass materialism, if applied thus without due qualification.

"IT IS NOT less true," pointed out Pope Pius XII, "that the root is deeper and more intrinsic, belonging to the sphere of religious belief and moral convictions which have been perverted by the progressive alienation of the peoples from that unity of doctrine, faith, customs, and morals which once was promoted by the tireless and beneficent work of the Church."

THE PROBLEM then is basically one of Christian education, or, as the same Pope tells us, of the "re-education of mankind" in "things spiritual and religious."

—FATHER G. JOSEPH GUSTAFSON, S.S.

August 27

"Judge not, that you be not judged. . . ."   —Matthew 7:1

SAINT FRANCIS DE SALES was a very wise man. He proved this in much of his homespun writing, even though his analogies seem incongruous in our fast-paced day.

AMONG THE WISEST things he wrote was his admonition that we should never call anyone a sinner unless we actually see him in the act of sinning and at the same time know the full state of his soul. That makes it rather difficult to call someone a sinner, does it not? Saint Francis goes on to make another serious point: too many of us refer to another in terms like, "Oh, he's a drunkard," or, "That woman has no morals," or, "That politician is a thief." Actually, in making such judgments, we may be accusing a saint—for if the person had repented even one moment before our accusation, he or she would be in the state of grace just as we were applying the label of sinner.

THE OBVIOUS moral is the one Jesus preached two thousands years ago: Do not judge other people.
                                              —FATHER DONALD F.X. CONNOLLY

August 28

Beloved, do not imitate evil but imitate good. He who does good is of God.   —3 John 11

SAINT AUGUSTINE is unquestionably one of the greatest saints, teachers, bishops, writers in the Church's long history. With all his great mind and ardent heart, he loved and served Christ once he found Him.

THE WRITINGS of St. Augustine are always modern for he wrote from the heart and on universal problems. Today he can help us to see the meaning of history in terms of the building of the City of God here on earth, that City which will be hidden and persecuted until Christ's glorious return.

LET US ASK St. Augustine to intercede for us for increased love of Christ and His Mystical Body, the Catholic Church; for greater devotion to the advancement of Christ's cause in our own family and neighborhood.
                                              —SISTER M. CHARLES BORROMEO, C.S.C.

August 29

He (Herod) sent and had John beheaded in the prison. . . .
—Matthew 14:10

O N this day John the Baptist graduated into heaven summa cum laude. To John, the most discerning judge of human nature paid the highest possible compliment: "He called him the greatest man born of woman."

FORTITUDE, then, must be among the virtues most highly prized by Christ, for it characterized the entire life of the Baptist. No reed shaken by the wind, John was able to endure the withering blasts and meager diet of the desert without complaint.

WITH UNWAVERING determination he preached the same message to peasants and soldiers, to Pharisees and kings. Called before Herod, who had absolute power over life and death, John could not dissemble. He condemned the immorality of the court, although he surely knew that such a forthright stand would cost him life itself. May we who have been so fickle, follow the example of his fortitude.

—FATHER FRANCIS R. MOESLEIN

August 30

"I have earnestly desired to eat this passover with you before I suffer."
—Luke 22:15

T HE elements of the Eucharist suggest a pattern we can follow in unifying the offering of all that we are and have to God in the formal worship of the Liturgy and the informal worship of the liturgy of daily life.

THE ELEMENTS are bread, made of individual grains of wheat baked together, and wine, from individual grapes crushed and fermented together. Before the consecration, they are just bread and wine. Afterwards, there is Jesus truly present in memorial-sacrifice in praise of the Father and for the dispensing of saving grace.

JUST as grains of wheat and separate grapes can be combined to form single substances, so can we combine all of the smallest and largest elements of our lives into a single offering of praise.

ALL OF IT takes in new significance when joined in quality and intention to the Person of Jesus Himself in sacrifice. The purpose of our life should be to make all of it good enough to be eucharistic.

—FATHER FELICIAN A. FOY, O.F.M.

August 31

The fruit of the righteous is a tree of life. —Proverbs 11:30

MOST of the Saints were specialists: there was something that they did well and into that framework they placed their dedication to the service of God. Some were preachers, some were mothers, some were writers, some were craftsmen, others lived a common life but well. St. Raymond Nonnatus put his dedication into the ransoming of slaves.

IN SEVERAL of his epistles St. Paul explained to the faithful that there are many places in the Mystical Body for various members of various talents and capacity. Everyone has his special place in the Church and his special function to perform. There is nothing to say that the only place that counts in the Church is at the altar or in the pulpit.

THERE IS SOMETHING that you do well. There is something that everyone can do, and none of these are short of dedication to the service of God who rarely calls any of us out of our accustomed ways. It is more common that He expects us to stay where we are, to be what we are and make that the avenue of our soul's salvation.

—MSGR. JAMES I. TUCEK

September 1

. . . This is only the beginning of what they will do; and nothing that they propose to do will be impossible for them.   —Genesis 11:6

SEPTEMBER! Can you believe it? Summer is almost gone and signs of fall are in the air. Vacation days are over and school has started. September is, in a way, a time of beginnings though it is so close to the end of the Church year and of the calendar year as well.

EVERY MONTH, every day is a time of new beginnings. Every day we tell ourselves that today, *this* day is going to be better than yesterday. We are going to keep those resolutions we are always making. We are going to go out of our way at work or school to be nice to that person who can be so irritable and seemingly unlovable. But we are going to keep reminding ourselves that God loves him/her. He had this person in mind from all eternity and called him/her out of nothingness as He called me.

BECAUSE of the human condition we will fail. We will not measure up. But we are not going to let this discourage us. We are not alone. The Holy Spirit is all-powerful. With God all things are possible.

—SISTER ELIZABETH ANN CLIFFORD, O.L.V.M.

September 2

Bless the Lord, winter cold and summer heat, sing praise to him and highly exalt him for ever.   —Daniel 3:43

YEARS ago, when I was a boy, I both loved and hated September. I hated it because summer was almost over and school was at hand; yet I loved it because nature's beauty still lingered and sparkled along the beaches and coves of my native Rhode Island.

LIFE has its share of memories or experiences like this that are bitter-sweet. We can't follow the endless summer, but have to return to school or work. Let it suffice to remember that God has given us the delights of the summer now fading, and for this we are grateful.

IF SCHOOL is difficult, or if our job puts heavy demands on us, then remember, too, that God has given us the brains, the steady hand, and the strong back to meet the challenge, and for this we are grateful, too.

—FATHER EDWIN R. MCDEVITT, M.M.

September 3

There is nothing better for a man than that he should eat and drink and find enjoyment in his toil. This also, I saw, is from the hand of God. —Ecclesiastes 2:24

THE dignity of work — Labor Day in America does not have the political overtone that May 1 has in Europe. We have always had a healthy respect for manual labor because we are not too distant from the pioneer days. Our forefathers carved a livelihood out of the hard earth by the sweat of their brow.

YET THERE is another aspect which gives work a still greater dignity. God wants man to collaborate with Him in finishing the world. He wants man to be a co-creator. The world has untold wealth, inexhaustible energy, and endless possibilities buried in her bosom.

ALL THIS is for man to discover, to bring to life, to bring under control, and to help serve man and thereby glorify God. This is the work of man. That work is most exalted.

—FATHER LOUIS J. PUTZ, C.S.C.

September 4

Teach me to do thy will, for thou art my God! Let thy good spirit lead me on a level path! —Psalms 143:10

A VERY important work assignment for many begins today, with the opening of school.

OUR HUMAN NATURE inclines so many of us to be impatient, especially in our youth. We just can't wait until we can enjoy the privileges of our older brothers and sisters—dating, driving, playing on the school athletic teams.

EVEN in later years, we find ourselves dreaming about the things we are going to accomplish in the future or the good we would do, if we had someone else's money or opportunities.

PLEASE help me God to see Your will for me today and to recognize the opportunities You give me to sanctify myself, if only I take advantage of them.

—FATHER JOHN R. MAGUIRE

September 5

For everything there is a season, and a time for every matter under heaven. —Ecclesiastes 3:1

GOD bestows a daily gift of Time. . . .
  . . . to reflect on His goodness
. . . to rejoice in His beautiful world
. . . to realize blessings given can be taken away
. . . to learn how to pray. (St. Teresa comforts us with: "I myself spent over fourteen years without ever being able to meditate except while reading.")
. . . to be thoughtful in home, office, school, community
. . . to withhold judgment and curb the tongue
. . . to laugh at ourselves
. . . to be compassionate toward the unlovely
. . . to fulfill duties, grateful for "a place to fill and work to do"
. . . to become a Listening Ear and Understanding Heart
. . . to age intellectually, spiritually, and with gentled disposition
. . . to love.

—MARION EGAN

September 6

"Go in peace, be warmed and filled." —James 2:16

THIS time between summer's sudden departure and autumn's gradual arrival, the days are usually pleasant and the sun shines a lot. I urge you to take time out to stand in that sun and caress its warmth. And then consider that one-syllable word: warmth.

CONSIDER the warmth of friendship; of a family-room fireplace when you're snow-soaked; of a real smile from the most unexpected person; of the June sun after a chilled swim; of a squeezed handclasp near your side; of a steaming tub after pulling weeds; of a homemade card from a child; of a letter from a friend when it's not even your birthday; of someone holding you close; of caring.

WARMTH is a good feeling both inside and out and its rays penetrate almost everyone's life, if you so desire. So, pile on another log and smile an extra smile, squeeze a hand, write a letter, care. Warmth is one of God's creations, both spiritually and physically. Embrace it.

—JO CURTIS DUGAN

September 7

I led them with cords of compassion, with the bands of love. . . .
—Hosea 11:4

A BOVE the Golden Dome of the main building of Notre Dame stands the statue of Our Lady, after whom the university is named. Thousands of students pray daily before her statue in the grotto, a replica of Lourdes.

MARY is the Patron of Youth, the Help of Christians and the Refuge of Sinners. Pray to her each day to obtain for you the graces needed for your station in life. She will never fail you.

A BEAUTIFUL custom for every Catholic family to observe is that of reciting, after the evening meal, the Family Rosary. Have each member take the lead in reciting a decade. Meditate carefully upon the mystery commemorated in each of the decades. In this way, the life of Christ and of His Blessed Mother will be kept vividly before your mind. Thus too will you receive the prayers and intercession of Our Blessed Mother.
—FATHER JOHN A. O'BRIEN

September 8

". . . Burn incense to the queen of heaven and pour out libations to her."
—Jeremiah 44:17

T ODAY is Our Lady's birthday. In our hearts let us repeat the words of the Office for the day: "Thy nativity, O Virgin Mother of God, has been a message of joy to the entire world."

ON THEIR birthdays we remember our living mothers with a gift or bouquet, and our deceased mothers with a spiritual bouquet of our prayers. So, in observance of her birthday, couldn't we give Our Heavenly Mother the gift of our hearts and the spiritual bouquet of our prayers and sacrifices?

ON THE birthday of our Queen surely there is something we can do to return, at least in some small measure, the love that Mary has for her subjects. Let us be as generous in giving to her as she has always shown herself to be in obtaining graces for us from her Son.
—FATHER ROBERT J. LEUVER, C.M.F.

September 9

The grace of the Lord Jesus Christ and the love of God and the fellowship of the Holy Spirit be with you all. —2 Corinthians 13:14

THE blessing given at the end of each Mass is a proclamation of belief in all that we have witnessed and shared. We make the sign of the cross as a sign of commitment that what we have heard spoken is the Word of God, and what we have just eaten is the Flesh and Blood of life itself.

WE HAVE begged forgiveness during the Mass and promised a change in our lives. We have professed our faith in a formal Creed and offered our lives as a testimony to our faith — Consecration, Communion — And finally, a thanksgiving for all the blessings and opportunities which are now ours.

THIS is what the blessing at the end of Mass signifies and seals. It admonishes us to "Go, *live* the Mass." Let it not be just a part of our day. Let it influence and take over our every action, our every word.

—JAMES MICHAEL SULLIVAN

September 10

"Peace be to you, and peace be to your house, and peace be to all that you have. . . ." —1 Samuel 25:6

I AM sure the greeting "Shalom" was often on Jesus' lips. It not only means peace but also wholeness and fullness. Shalom hopes the very best for a person. It is difficult for us to enjoy everyone but we can hope that they receive the best of what life offers.

CARDINAL SUENENS described the full meaning of Shalom when he said: "The greatest good we can do for others is not to give them of our wealth but to show them their own."

SHALOM brings us beyond the horizon of our own ideas and idiosyncrasies. We begin to tolerate other people. We do not attempt to form them into our shadow. We encourage them to develop their own talents. They have a fullness and potential all of their own. We might not agree with their ideas or life-style but at least we are happy that they are becoming themselves.

—FATHER JOHN C. TORMEY

September 11

"You shall not wrong a stranger or oppress him. . . ."

—Exodus 22:21

COURTESY, springs from a deep respect for a person as created by God, loved by God and redeemed by Christ, as we all are.

A FRIGID politeness that satisfies the conventions but makes another feel embarrassed or inferior is an insult to God and man.

THERE ARE occasions when you feel justified in giving the polite brush-off and the frozen mitt to people who bore you with their trivialities or hang on interminably, wasting your precious time. Yet the true Christian, however busy, always seems, somehow to find time to be kind to people and make them feel welcome. The fact that he's the same to everyone isn't an artificial show of politeness. On the contrary, it's genuine Christian courtesy that makes him lay aside all else to devote his whole attention and consideration to his fellow-creature who is, by God's will, with him at that moment.

—FATHER GORDON ALBION

September 12

By the grace of God I am what I am, and his grace toward me was not in vain. 1 Corinthians 15:10

THE striking catch of fishes moves Simon Peter, the impulsive disciple to adore the Master Who had wrought the miracle.

THE THOUGHT of Paul calls attention to that profound penetration and progress in faith which is rather the fruit of prayer. Only gradually does our prayer — our prayer for others and theirs for us — combined with a life of virtue bring us closer to God. Only gradually do we pass spiritually from the darkness of incipient faith to light as we enter more deeply into the Kingdom of God's beloved Son. Then indeed will we belong entirely to Him who is the Head of all Creation: the result will be true and abiding reconciliation with God and the peace which Jesus has earned for us through the Blood of His Cross.

LET US frequently reflect on progress in faith through prayer and good works. This is a resolution we should make at the beginning of this autumn month. The surest way to remain steadfast in the life of faith is to make constant progress day by day in love of the Savior.

—FATHER EDWIN G. KAISER, C.PP.S.

September 13

". . . Indeed, the hour is coming when whoever kills you will think he is offering a service to God. . . ." —John 16:2

TODAY'S Saint (St. John Chrysostom) was called the "golden mouthed" because of his extraordinary eloquence. He was given charge of the Church of Constantinople. He strongly deplored and opposed the licentiousness of the nobility and was subjected to hatred and finally to exile. He died in 407.

OUR LORD foretold that those who followed Him could expect suffering. "If the world hates you, know that it has hated me before it hated you. . . . If they persecuted me, they will persecute you . . ." (John 15:18-20).

THE LITANY of the Saints and the book of life are filled with the names of canonized and uncanonized men and women whose moral integrity and loyalty to Christ have been and are a standing indictment of the immorality of our age. And they are suffering as Christ predicted. They are ridiculed for their virtue, pitied for their childish spirituality, looked upon as sacrificial fools. They suffer this because they know their dedication brings the blessing of God who is purity itself.

—FATHER MAURUS FITZGERALD, O.F.M.

September 14

"If any man would come after me, let him deny himself and take up his cross and follow me." —Matthew 16:24

EXALTATION of the Holy Cross — If you drag your cross reluctantly it will scrape wearily along the ground and bite deeply into your shoulder. The looser you hold it, the heavier it is.

BUT IF YOU embrace it, if you lift it willingly, half the burden will be gone. In that sense a cross is like an anchor. The boat can carry it and never know it is there, but it cannot drag it without feeling the strain.

ONE GOOD WAY to look at the Cross is not to remember what the Cross has done to you, but rather what it has done *for* you. Think of the good things that never would have come into your life, if trouble had not opened the door: the people you never would have met, the prayers you never would have said, the merit you never would have built up — if Our Savior had not beckoned you closer to Him, on the Cross.

—FATHER JOSEPH E. MANTON, C.SS.R.

September 15

Oh Mary, Mediatrix and Co-redemptrix . . . pray for us!

SEVEN Sorrows of Mary — Seven Sorrows there were, which stabbed the heart of Mary! Other painful and anxious moments could no doubt be listed, but these seven could be experienced by no other human . . . for Mary was the Mother of God and her sorrow was inflicted on her by what the sins of man would do to her Son.

> Simeon's Prophecy
> Flight into Egypt
> Loss in the Temple
> Meeting Jesus on Way to Calvary
> Crucifixion of Jesus
> Removal from the Cross
> Burial of Jesus

THERE WAS NO selfish sorrow in Mary. She could think only of her Son. It was the events in Christ's life, her Son, her flesh and blood, that caused her pain . . . and this only because she willed to be a part of her Son in His Redemptive life.

WASTE NO time on useless self-pity!
— BISHOP ALBERT R. ZUROWESTE, Belleville, Illinois

September 16

If we have died with him, we shall also live with him.
— 2 Timothy 2:11

A YOUNG flier, killed during World War II, had time before he died to scrawl only a few words as a final message to his parents. The note read:

"DEAR MOM and pop: I had time to say my prayers. Jack."

NO FAREWELL note could be much shorter, yet few could be more reassuring to truly Christian parents. To them this little message was the news of their son's eternal happiness and the heartening reward of their own teaching, that his last thought should have been to pray.

SOME PARENTS think of their responsibilities to their children chiefly in material terms. More important is the care of their souls. Proper example in early life can do much to set them on the true path.

— FATHER JAMES KELLER, M.M.

September 17

In this is love perfected with us, that we may have confidence for the day of judgment, because as he is so are we in this world.
—1 John 4:17

IN this ecumenical age some of us are inclined to ignore the great truth enunciated by the Second Vatican Council that the Church of Christ subsists in the Roman Catholic Church. St. Robert Bellarmine was probably the greatest defender of the truth of the Church in our modern age. His vast grasp of the Sacred Scriptures, of tradition, and the History of the Church, his clear and well-ordered mind, and deep spirit of faith enabled him to organize his writings at a time when the defense of the truth was in a very chaotic state.

THOUGH we may not at all be able to imitate such great works as St. Robert's *Controversies,* with its powerful synthesis of Protestant and Catholic doctrine, we can in some measure study the doctrine of the Church from more readily available sources. Thus we should be able to instruct our children and even many others who are grasping for the truth. But we can always imitate the Saint in our loyalty to the Church.

—FATHER EDWIN G. KAISER, C.PP.S.

September 18

The grass is gone, and the new growth appears, and the herbage of the mountains is gathered. . . . —Proverbs 27:25

SEPTEMBER is a month for deep thinking. It is too late for new planting. Nature sends its blooms forth only in spring, to be matured into fruit and vegetables during the summer and harvested in the fall. There is an inexorable rhythm in this.

NOTHING CAN be harvested from what has not been planted and nurtured. Hard labor of the spring can likewise be lost for want of summer rain, by the descent of an early frost or freeze.

PROMISES CANNOT always be fulfilled, nor the harvests of desire reaped. This is a part of the education of life. Degrees are not always earned nor awarded for how much knowledge has been acquired, but rather by how well it has been applied to the art of living, the quality of acceptance of what God has permitted. For some a little is a fortune, for others no fortune is enough.

—ANNE TANSEY

September 19

We have aimed to please those who wish to read, to make it easy for those wo are inclined to memorize, and to profit all readers.
— 2 Maccabees 2:25

IF the body needs regular food, this is no less true of the mind. Reading serves that purpose. There was a time when few people could read and when books were very expensive. Now it is everybody's birthright to learn to read.

YOU CAN'T always choose your neighbors, but you can choose your friends in the books you select for reading. If it is true that you can tell a man by the company he keeps, it is more true that you can judge a person by the kind of reading he does. After all, reading is the finest and most powerful way of influencing a person's thinking. There is a book at the source of every great movement in history. We should learn to grow in wisdom.

— FATHER LOUIS J. PUTZ, C.S.C.

September 20

Above all these put on love, which binds everything together in perfect harmony. —Colossians 3:14

SOON after Pius XII was elected Pope in 1939, he called for charity.

"IT IS your divine call to open hearts to the love and grace of Jesus Christ," he wrote, "but this love should be kindled in you first by union with Christ in prayer and sacrifice. We say in union of prayer: If you ask us for a watchword . . . we answer, Pray, pray ever more frequently.

"IN UNION of sacrifice: Not only in the Eucharistic sacrifice, but in that of ourselves . . . There are various forms of Christian asceticism, but none offers a road to divine charity apart from self-sacrifice. This is what Jesus Christ expects of His followers."

AT PENTECOST two years later, Pius XII emphasized Christian social charity: "Keep burning the noble flame of a brotherly social spirit . . . Do not allow it to go unkindled . . . Nourish it, keep it alive, increase it . . . Carry it wherever a groan of suffering, a lament of misery, a cry of pain reaches you; feed it ever more with the heat of a love drawn from the Heart of your Redeemer."

— FATHER JOHN J. CONSIDINE, M.M.

September 21

Jesus said to him: "Follow me." —Matthew 9:9

SAINT Matthew, whose feast we celebrate today, was a Jewish publican, and a tax gatherer for Rome. Since no one likes to pay taxes, he was not exactly popular. He was, however, an astute man of the world, the exact opposite, in character and training, of the simple fishermen, Simon, Andrew, James, and John, whose company he joined at the call of Christ. When Christ said to him, "Follow me," Matthew got up from his toll table and immediately followed Him.

THERE IS something supremely dramatic about his instant response, as there was in the response of Peter, Andrew, James, and John, when at Jesus' call, they left their large fishing boats and valuable nets and followed Him.

THERE IS much virtue in a wholehearted, eager, loving response. It won for the Apostles a wonderful new life in the company of the Savior of the World. It could mean a new beginning for each of us.

—FATHER MAURUS FITZGERALD, O.F.M.

September 22

Put on then . . . holy and beloved, compassion, kindness, lowliness, meekness, and patience. —Colossians 3:12

IN WILL ROGERS' humor there was usually an element of sober, down to earth truth. At times he startled his listeners by the shrewdness of his insight into human nature. On one occasion he said:

"SO LIVE THAT YOU wouldn't be ashamed to sell the family parrot to the town gossip."

THERE ARE MANY reasons for practicing kindness on all occasions, even in the secrecy of your home. Fear of what others may think of you is often a restraint. But it is far better to be motivated by a higher purpose.

THE MORE YOU grow in love of people, the less likelihood there is that you will hurt anyone in your family circle, or anywhere, for that matter.

—FATHER JAMES KELLER, M.M.

September 23

"I will quietly look from my dwelling like clear heat in sunshine, like a cloud of dew in the heat of harvest." —Isaiah 18:4

FALL has officially arrived. Some of you live farther north than we do and the leaves are already turning red and gold. It will be a few more weeks before our Wabash River Valley is aflame. What a beautiful sight it is when the maples, the oaks, the elms, and all our trees are a blaze of color, color that makes the spruces and cedars look greener than ever.

THE WILLOWS first turn yellow, then a deeper and deeper gold. Like the oaks they are reluctant to shed their leaves. But after the other trees reach their peak, the willow leaves begin to fade and to fall. Yet, as you drive along the road, you are surprised to see a maple still aflame though all around it are other maples naked and leafless.

IT IS THE SAME with people. Why it is that some continue to bloom, to stand out from the others, we cannot understand. It is one of God's many secrets. But even though we might not be so vigorous in appearance as the lone maple, we can still be strong in our spiritual life, in our life of union with God.

—SISTER ELIZABETH ANN CLIFFORD, O.L.V.M.

September 24

I call upon God; and the Lord will save me. Evening and morning and at noon I utter my complaint and moan, and he will hear my voice. —Psalms 55:16-17

GENERAL CHARLES GORDON of England had the daily practice of placing a white handkerchief outside the door of his tent in the southern Sudan. Every soldier knew that it meant the general was spending a half hour in prayer.

WE ALL NEED to fix a definite time to spend with God in prayer. It is the most precious period of our day.

ONE of the simplest and most beautiful of all prayers is the Sign of the Cross. In it we express our belief in one God in three divine Persons and show our belief in the Redemption by tracing with our hand the figure of a cross upon us. Say that simple prayer slowly, devoutly and with great reverence and it will thereby kindle the devotion in all the prayers which follow.

—FATHER JOHN A. O'BRIEN

September 25

"You shall love the Lord your God with all your heart, and with all your soul, and with all your strength, and with all your mind; and your neighbor as yourself." —Luke 10:27

IN days wherein the right answers seem to be few and far between, the one everlasting truth that lies at the basis of all religion, peace and happiness, remains steadfast. A lawyer asked the question for the first time, perhaps seeking some novel step to take, some new shrine to be visited or some person to consult in order to be saved. But he already knew the only answer to the all-important question.

THE TRUTH is found in the law . . . the law of love.

LOVE fulfills every law. With love every obligation is accomplished, without love, none.

—BISHOP ALBERT R. ZUROWESTE, Belleville, Illinois

September 26

Give thanks to the Lord, for he is good, for his mercy endures for ever. —Daniel 3:67

WE live in a wonderful age. Scientists call it the "Space Age." Man has broken out of this enclosed little world of ours and plunged into outer space. We are growing almost casual about Explorers in orbit over our heads and Telestar relaying pictures to our TV sets. And soon, man will be attempting interplanetary landings.

WE MAY forget that there was another time-space breakthrough 2,000 years ago which was much more important and earth-shaking. Only this breakthrough came from the other side. It was not man plunging into outer space, but God coming out of eternity into time.

IT WAS when God broke through into this world of ours—"And the Word was made flesh and dwelt amongst us." He came to teach us how to live and how to love. Since then human living has become simplified. It is simply being Christlike.

—FATHER JOSEPH F. HOGAN, S.J.

September 27

The poor will never cease out of the land; therefore I command you,
You shall open wide your hand to your brother, to the needy and to
the poor, in the land. —Deuteronomy 15:11

VINCENT DE PAUL (1581-1660) is uniquely associated with works of charity. Not mystical nor even profoundly theological, but deeply spiritual, he permitted no opportunity to help the poor and needy to escape him. Truly the Father of the Poor, he has been officially declared the Patron of works of charity by the Church. He is the Founder of the first Confraternity of Charity, an association of pious laywomen who assist the poor and the sick. He sought to alleviate the sad plight of the galley slaves, founded the Society of the Missions (the Vincentians), composed the rule for the Daughters of Charity, was their Superior General. Most interested in students for the priesthood, he founded seminaries.

TOUCHING was his love for foundlings, despised and neglected by the lofty and haughty ladies of the time. He is our great ideal for the love and concern for the ghettoes, for all our problems of charity. He stressed what we are likely most to overlook: the divine, the Christ, in the lowliest of men and women.
—FATHER EDWIN G. KAISER, C.PP.S.

September 28

. . . Humility goes before honor. —Proverbs 15:33

FRANK DUFF, the founder of the Legion of Mary, once said: "Humility is all too often a pious excuse for laziness."

ESPECIALLY in his work with the organizations for the ladies, the priest has a very difficult time convincing some members to accept an office. "There are so many members of this organization who are more capable than I." "I didn't have much training in school and was married before I could get some experience in the business world."

IF WE would just do the very best we can to fulfill a responsibility and then let the rest to God, there would be many more fine officers in our Catholic organizations. Also, in the case of the ladies, we would have healthier wives and mothers. As children grow more able to care for themselves, a little responsibility is the best medicine to assure a lady of her worth and avoid possible emotional problems.
—FATHER JOHN R. MAGUIRE

September 29

"Truly, truly, I say to you, you will see heaven opened, and the angels of God ascending and descending upon the Son of man." —John 1:51

TODAY is the feast of the Archangels — Saints Michael, Gabriel and Raphael. Preoccupied as we are with sending men to the moon and hurling satellites into space, do we ever give thought to God's messengers, the Angels? Our concern with what is limited and tangible should not shut out consideration of the angelic world that is unlimited and intangible.

SCRIPTURE is full of references to Angels and their loving concern for men. The compassionate story of the Archangel Raphael, guiding and counseling the youthful Tobias, is proof that we have friends whom we see not.

HOW LONG has it been since we thought of or took heed of the gentle promptings of Our Guardian Angel? He is a reminder that we are both God's creatures destined through difficulties to move on to glory.

—FATHER EDWIN R. MCDEVITT, M.M.

September 30

I commend you because you remember me in everything and maintain the traditions even as I have delivered them to you.
—1 Corinthians 11:2

ON this last day of September thank God for whatever good He has sent you, materially and spiritually. As for the difficult times, question if you will, but hold no bitterness. Question prayerfully, asking God to gift you with a better understanding of His ways. Ask for strengthened faith, renewed hope, repeat your trust in Him. Recognize again your nothingness and His all, but recognize, too, His total understanding and compassion.

IF YOU are discouraged, kneel at God's feet today and talk to Him about you in September, . . . your fears, your hopes, your weaknesses, your love for Him. He will listen. All-knowing. He understands your human failings; He understands your human feelings. He is your best friend. Count on Him.

REFRESHED, re-read the reflection for September 1 and welcome October with new zeal and determination. Pick yourself up, and begin again. You are going in the right direction.

—JO CURTIS DUGAN

October 1

"You are the light of the world. . . ." —Matthew 5:14

OCTOBER is dedicated to the Queen of the Holy Rosary. And what is the Rosary? It is a form of prayer in which beads are passed between the fingers. The Apostles' Creed is said while holding the Crucifix, the Our Father is said on the large beads, and the Hail Mary is said on the small beads. After each group of Hail Marys, one says "Glory be to the Father."

WHILE SAYING the "decades" of Hail Marys, we generally meditate on some mystery from the life of Our Lord or His Blessed Mother. (The following pages will suggest some thoughts for these reflections.)

THE BEADS are a tangible means of keeping our minds on God and His Blessed Mother. Just to touch them in our purse or pocket is like putting our hand for a moment in hers. The Rosary has been called a bouquet of fresh, fragrant flowers culled from the human heart.

—FATHER PATRICK PEYTON, C.S.C.

October 2

He will give his angels charge of you to guard you in all your ways. —Psalms 91:11

ANGELS played a part in the public life of Our Lord. In the desert, after the forty days of prayer and fasting, His first encounter with the prince of darkness followed. After the devil had left Him, "angels came and ministered to Him." In the agony in the Garden, when His time of trial was most grievous, an angel from Heaven stood by Him and gave Him strength.

SOMETIMES the Good News is almost too good to be true. An angel has a part in the life of each of us! The readings of today's Mass remind us that an angel guardian is assigned to each of us for the duration of our life. This benefit is ours because we are human beings with an eternal destiny. The only effective obstacle to our angel's guarding love is our own intellect and will. We ourselves can defeat that guardianship; and we do so in every sin.

WHEN did you last think of or pray to your Guardian Angel?
—FATHER THOMAS M. BREW, S.J.

October 3

And he came and preached peace to you who were far off and peace to those who were near. —Ephesians 2:17

O N October 4, 1965 Pope Paul VI made an impassioned plea for peace before the most impressive group of representatives ever assembled in history. Who could forget the urgency in his voice: "War never again!" He indicated that peace would only come through responding to the best within ourselves, through obeying God's Law.

BUT PEOPLE never listen to prophets, and peace is still fragile today in so many areas of the world, even among Christians.

IF OUR faith doesn't warn us of the danger of war, let the reality and power of modern weapons warn us. John Kennedy put it very starkly: "Mankind must put an end to war or war will put an end to mankind."

—REV. MR. PETER M. STRAVINSKAS

October 4

Great peace have those who love thy law; nothing can make them stumble. —Psalms 119:165

T HE virtues of humility and simplicity shine forth in the life of Saint Francis of Assisi who stands before us in the liturgy of today. Even though you may know the prayer of Saint Francis, each rereading reveals hidden treasures.

Lord make me an instrument of Thy *peace.*
Where there is hatred let me sow *love;*
Where there is injury, *pardon;*
Where there is doubt, *faith;*
Where there is despair, *hope;*
Where there is darkness, *light;*
And where there is sadness, *joy.*
O Divine Master, grant that I may not so much seek to be consoled, as to *console;*
To be understood, as to *understand;*
To be loved, as to *love;*
For it is in giving that we *receive;*
It is in pardoning that we are *pardoned;*
And it is in dying that we are born to *eternal life.*

RESOLVE: To be an instrument of such peace!
—BISHOP JOHN J. CARBERRY, Lafayette-in-Indiana

October 5

I have seen the business that God has given to the sons of men to be busy with. He has made everything beautiful in its time.
—Ecclesiastes 3:10-11

THE range and richness of nature's color during October reminds us that the Church has its own rich, colorful season this month.

SAINTS abound in fascinating variety: The Little Flower, Francis of Assisi, Edward the Confessor, Luke the Evangelist, Teresa the Mystic.

BUT for generations October means the Rosary — a renewed fervor in saying it, a greater awareness of its spiritual riches.

GOOD Pope John wrote early in his pontificate: "In reciting the Rosary, the thing that matters is devoutly meditating on each mystery as we move our lips. Therefore, we are sure that our children and all their brethren throughout the world will turn it into a school for learning true perfection, as with a deep spirit of recollection, they contemplate the teachings that shine forth from the life of Christ and of Mary Most Holy."
—FATHER FRANCIS X. CANFIELD

October 6

For where your treasure is, there will your heart be also.
—Luke 12:34

WHEN a distinguished visitor to the Vatican asked Pope Pius XI what was the most valuable treasure there, the Pope drew from his pocket a well-worn Rosary, pointed to it, and said, "This is the greatest treasure anywhere."

AT LOURDES, Our Lady appeared some eighteen times and invited Bernadette to say the Rosary with her. In the six appearances at Fatima, Our Lady insisted on the recitation of the Rosary.

AT FATIMA, Mary identified herself, saying "I am the Lady of the Rosary, and I have come to warn the faithful to amend their lives and ask pardon for their sins. . . . They must say the Rosary."

THROUGH the Rosary today, as in past times of peril that have threatened civilization, Mary has again come to save men from the evils that overwhelm them. Are you faithful to the daily recitation of the Rosary? Begin today, while there is still time.
—MSGR. CHARLES HUGO DOYLE

October 7

. . . And when the Lord has dealt with my lord, then remember your handmaid. —1 Samuel 25:31

IF all the facts could be written about the blessings which have come to mankind through the centuries as a result of the Rosary, many libraries would have to be devoted exclusively to such writings. God alone knows what to us are the countless extraordinary favors given to those who implored Mary's help through the Rosary.

NOT A DAY PASSES BY — in fact, not even an hour — when special blessings are not being bestowed upon individuals who are praying their Rosaries to seek assistance from Our Blessed Mother.

THE ROSARY — embracing as it does the Apostles' Creed, the Our Father, the Hail Mary with its angelic salutation and the request for the continued prayer of the Blessed Mother for one's needs now and at the hour of death, and the Glory to the Three Persons of the Trinity — is packed with the power that moves heaven to right the wrongs on earth.

—MSGR. RALPH G. KUTZ

October 8

Let us then with confidence draw near to the throne of grace, that we may receive mercy and find grace to help in time of need.
—Hebrews 4:16

THE Lord tells us that we should strive after God-like perfection. "Be ye perfect as also your heavenly Father is perfect." A casual consideration of this advice would tend to make us think that the Lord is expecting too much from frail human beings. Deeper reflection, however, prompts us to realize that the Lord would never counsel anything that was beyond human potential.

IT MUST be possible, therefore, for us to develop God-like qualities and attributes. Which? Certainly not His omniscience or omnipotence; His knowledge of all things or His power over the whole universe.

BUT HOW about His kindness, mercy, compassion, forgiveness, patience? These qualities are definitely within our ability to foster and develop. If perfected they could easily furnish us with a God-like image much to the satisfaction of those around us and a delight to the angels and saints.

—BISHOP ANDREW G. GRUTKA, Gary, Indiana

October 9

Jesus said to them, "Render to Caesar the things that are Caesar's, and to God the things that are God's." —Mark 12:17

THIS scriptural quotation is not a direct reply to the question of paying taxes. Yet, Jesus certainly implies there is an area for the legitimate exercise of political power. Peter and Paul recognized this legitimacy in their writings. So it can be said that the Gospel proclaims the separation of Church and State.

BUT the psalm declares the supremacy of God, "You families of nations, give to the Lord glory and praise . . . the Lord is king." This proclamation of God's glory, the primacy of His Word, has meant conflict with the State as in our day when the right of abortion is said to be the law of the land.

AS ST. PAUL urges his first European converts, the Thessalonians, so must we show in our daily lives and actions the reality of our faith and never lose hope in Our Lord Jesus Christ. No matter how great the opposition, God's providence directs all things as in Isaiah: "I am the Lord and there is no other, there is no God besides me."

—FATHER GEORGE M. BUCKLEY, M.M.

October 10

Bless the Lord, nights and days, sing praise to him and exalt him for ever. —Daniel 3:47

WITH October the fall season begins to move in upon us in earnest. Living green gives way to dying brown, the lush foliage of the spring and summer will soon be gone and will be replaced by the threadbare limbs of winter.

BUT FALL AIR produces a quickening tempo and a flow of energy as well as drying leaves. Fall and winter come into our lives in the form of troubles and difficulties just as rhythmically as they march behind each other in their seasonal forms.

WE ARE CONSTANTLY being challenged by adversities. Will we sit and stare at the dying leaves of our life or will we respond with renewed energy and confidence?

—FATHER JOHN MCCARTHY

October 11

Train up a child in the way he should go, and when he is old he will not depart from it. —Proverbs 22:6

CAN we ever forget the days of our childhood when we begged favors with an almost badgering persistence? The persistence of a child who wishes to obtain a favor from his mother is much to be admired and even imitated. A child is never satisfied with an outright "no" answer. He realizes that with each petition for a favor, the likelihood of obtaining that favor (or another one in its place) is strengthened.

CAN OUR Mother fail to give ear to the precious persistence of her children when they devoutly recite her Rosary? And if the particular favor we seek is not granted, can we not be certain that Mary will reward our perseverance by asking her Divine Son to grant us another favor more in keeping with our total spiritual welfare?

IF YOU have not in the past been faithful to the devout recitation of the Rosary, then begin at once. If you have been faithful to this magnificent prayer, then rest assured that you are a child of Mary.

—FATHER LEON MCKENZIE

October 12

He who does not take his cross and follow me is not worthy of me. —Matthew 10:38

HERE is one temptation experienced by the great St. Teresa of Avila, which has a certain timeliness in our neurotic age. We advise you to see your doctor if necessary, but then to take these wise words to heart after that. We are all in God's hands.

"AS MY OWN health is so bad, I was always impeded by my fears, and my devotion was of no value at all until I resolved not to worry any more about my body or my health; and now I trouble about them very little. For it pleased God to reveal to me this device of the devil; and so, whenever the devil suggested that I should ruin my health, I would reply: 'Even if I die is of little consequence.' 'Rest, indeed!' I would say. 'I need no rest; what I need is crosses.' "

IF ONLY we would follow her advice, we would never have to fear an ulcer and half the world's psychiatrists would be out of business.

—FATHER G. JOSEPH GUSTAFSON, S.S.

October 13

. . . Grace is poured upon your lips. —Psalms 45:2

THE toast seems to be a universal custom. Englishmen say "cheers," and Frenchmen, "to your health," and the Swedes say, "Skol." The sip from the wine glass preludes joy, just as the gulp from the medicine bottle anticipates a growl of misery. In the magic rites of ancient times, people drank variously from the cup of happiness and the chalice of bitterness.

THE BIBLE frequently uses this image. The clergy spoke of divine displeasure in the cup (Deuteronomy 15:23). But Jesus at the Last Supper drank from the cup of blessing and heavenly happiness. He was on His way to glory, though reminding His followers that a cup of sorrow precedes the glorification.

THE CUP of blessing at the Lord's Supper was a sign of cheer as well as a pledge of pain. Christian life is still that inevitable mixture of death and resurrection sustained by the final vision of a toast in the kingdom.

—FATHER ALFRED A. MCBRIDE, O. PRAEM.

October 14

God is our refuge and strength, a very present help in trouble.
—Psalms 46:1

KEEP me going, Lord! There is a little wall plaque in our kitchen which reads: Keep Me Going, Lord. Maybe it doesn't sound like a prayer, but it is. For a tired and harried mother, it reminds her of her dependence on the Blessed Lord. For the tired and worried father, it is a reminder that every man wearies and falters at times.

FOR ALL who view the words, it is a witness that without God's help, we really can't do anything.

FOR EVERY good and every perfect gift comes from Him whether He gets the credit from us or not. And, all that we are or ever hope to be will come ultimately from Him, the Father of us all. For in Him we live and move and have our being.

—MRS. BETTY J. HAYES

October 15

. . . The bridegroom came, and those who were ready went in with him to the marriage feast. . . . —Matthew 25:10

ST. TERESA of Avila is one of the most remarkable women of all time. She and St. Catherine of Siena are the first two women ever to be officially declared Doctors of the Church. In a rare way, St. Teresa of Avila combined the life of religious contemplation with an intense activity and commonsense efficiency in practical affairs.

THIS contemplative-in-action was occupied for twenty years with the reform of Carmel and the establishment of eighteen new foundations all over Spain. Constant traveling, difficult negotiations with civil and Church authorities, worries about building and organization, responsibilities of administration and religious guidance, a huge correspondence and the writing of books that are masterpieces, were all accomplished without harm to her inner life.

SAINTS also show us how to depart this life. When death was near and Viaticum was brought to Teresa, she exclaimed: "Bridegroom and Lord, the longed-for hour has come! It is time for us to see one another. It is time for me to set out. Let us go. . . ."

—FATHER THOMAS M. BREW, S.J.

October 16

"The harvest is past, the summer is ended. . . ." —Jeremiah 8:20

OCTOBER, the height of fall, presents a magnificent spectacle to our view. The fields are rich with their harvest, and the leaves on the trees are splashed with color. As John Donne wrote, "No spring, no summer beauty hath such grace as I have seen in one autumnal face."

THE BOUNTY of the harvest and the brilliance of the forest manifest the goodness and beauty of their Creator. "Since the creation of the world, invisible realities, God's eternal power and divinity, have become visible, recognized through the things He has made" (Romans 1:20).

AUTUMN is an ideal time to pause in our work and do some contemplating. Nature's scenes make us more sensitive to the providence and the presence of God. Gathering fruits from the field gives us a chance to glimpse the fruits we have reaped so far from our lives.

—FATHER ALBERT CYLWICKI

October 17

Be faithful unto death, and I will give you the crown of life. —Revelation 2:10

LESS than a hundred years after the death and resurrection of Christ, Ignatius of Antioch died a martyr's death in Rome during the reign of the Emperor Trajan. He is remembered for the warm and instructive letters he wrote to the Churches of Asia Minor and to the Church of Rome while on his journey to martyrdom, for him the supreme way of imitating Christ. He writes, "May nothing seen or unseen fascinate me, so that I may happily make my way to Christ! Fire, cross, struggles with wild beasts, wrenching of bones, mangling of limbs, crunching of the whole body, cruel tortures inflicted by the devil — let them come upon me, provided I make my way to Jesus Christ."

BUT HIS spirituality was not an individualistic thing. His letters are one of the few early witnesses outside the New Testament to the basic teachings of our Catholic faith: to the central place of the bishop in his diocese and the primacy of the Bishop of Rome. These are now severely challenged. Saint Ignatius pray for the Church today!

—FATHER GEORGE M. BUCKLEY, M.M.

October 18

. . . It seemed good to me also, having followed all things closely for some time past, to write an orderly account for you . . . that you may know the truth concerning the things of which you have been informed. —Luke 1:3-4

NO one would fail to recognize St. Luke as one of the four Evangelists but many of us do forget from time to time the style and the accent that is to be found in St. Luke's Gospel. Just as Matthew went out of his way to write for the Jewish people and to point out how Our Lord had fulfilled Old Testament prophecy so also St. Luke stressed that Christ had come for all people, Gentiles as well as Jews.

ST. LUKE loves to stress and to point out the gentleness of Christ in His concern for suffering.

WE CAN well afford to apply the general themes of St. Luke's Gospel in our daily life. This is Christ's concern for all men and His alleviation of suffering.

—FATHER JOHN MCCARTHY

October 19

Though I walk in the midst of trouble, thou dost preserve my life; thou dost stretch out thy hand against the wrath of my enemies, and the right hand delivers me. —Psalms 138:7

THE watchful servants of today's Gospel are exemplified in today's saints, the North American martyrs. Over three hundred years ago, these eight French Jesuit missionaries became the first to attain the martyr's crown in North America. One of them, Isaac Jogues, a man of learning and culture, gave up a teaching career in his native country to work among the Indians in the New World.

FATHER JOGUES was captured by the Iroquois and imprisoned for thirteen months during which he and his companions were beaten and tortured. The Dutch of Fort Orange helped him to escape and return to France. Because several of his fingers had been cut or burnt off by the Indians, Pope Urban VIII gave him permission to offer Mass with his mutilated hands. Instead of remaining at home, he soon returned to his mission — and martyrdom.

—FATHER THOMAS M. BREW, S.J.

October 20

Take my yoke upon you, and learn from me; for I am gentle and lonely in heart, and you will find rest for your souls. —Matthew 11:29

SAINT JOSEPH shares with Our Lady the special tribute during the month of October. Following is a simple (but be assured difficult) novena in his honor which has been found to be so efficacious that one is advised to be sure that one really wants what one asks for.

IT CONSISTS in turning to Saint Joseph four times a day (it does not matter when or where) and considering *for a minute* on each visit these qualities:
His Fidelity to Grace;
His Fidelity to the Interior Life;
His Love of Our Blessed Lady;
His love for the Holy Child.

NO SPECIAL prayers are required. You do the thinking and the praying; you reflect upon, e.g., the fidelity of Saint Joseph to Grace for a minute, thank God for this quality in him, and ask that you may likewise be faithful.

—BISHOP JOHN J. CARBERRY, Lafayette-in-Indiana

October 21

Do not be led away by diverse and strange teachings; for it is well that the heart be strengthened by grace, not by foods. . . . —Hebrews 13:9

EVERY event in the life of Jesus came about by the express decree or by the permission of God. The same is true of all events in our own lives — that included in which the human element is most apparent. Jesus is my Model.

DO I PRAY for grace to forgive what I cannot forget? Do I practice self-control when I feel hurt? Do I make allowances for mistakes and misunderstanding and strive to accommodate myself to those of a different character from my own? Am I as quick to excuse others as I do myself?

"O MY PEOPLE, what have I done to thee, or in what have I molested thee? Answer thou me!" O my King, can I resist this piteous sight! Can I see unmoved what my sins have brought upon Thee!

THIS is expiation of my evil thoughts; my pride, rebellion, uncharitable interpretation! This is the treatment He receives from His children! This to teach me how to bear anxiety.
—BISHOP REMBERT C. KOWALSKI, O.F.M., Wuchang, China

October 22

May the God of hope fill you with all joy and peace in believing, so that by the power of the Holy Spirit you may abound in hope. —Romans 15:13

FROM the moment of His conception in Mary's womb, Jesus enjoyed the serene bliss of the Beatific Vision. Although He would live a very down-to-earth life, His earth was a heaven because He always saw His Father face-to-face. That is why the soul of Christ did not have the virtue of hope.

HOPE IS ONLY the earth-covered root of heavenly possession, and Jesus possessed His Father from the first. *Mary's* hope, then, is the most perfect ever bestowed on a human soul.

THE CHURCH CALLS MARY the Mother of Sacred Hope. She is the most exalted model of perfect confidence in God. Hail Holy Queen, our life, our sweetness, and our hope! After this, our exile, show unto us the blessed Fruit of thy womb, Jesus.
—FATHER PATRICK PEYTON, C.S.C.

October 23

He brought them out of darkness and gloom, and broke their bonds asunder. —Psalms 107:14

WHEN Captain James E. Ray came home from his isolation in a Vietnam war prison, in 1973, he recalled this experience: "For some reason I suddenly felt I wasn't alone. I don't know whether it was the power of prayer or an intervention by God."

CAPTAIN Jeremiah A. Denton described how he endured a prison torture rig: "I simply told God He would just have to take over. I had reached the end. As soon as I got that prayer out, this mantle of comfort came over me and I couldn't feel any more pain."

THESE experiences remind us of Abraham. "Abraham never questioned or doubted God's promise; rather he was strengthened in faith and gave glory to God, fully persuaded that God could do whatever He had promised" (Romans 4).

THE LORD has promised that He will be with us during our darkest hours. If we never doubt His presence, there is no difficulty we cannot endure. If we are fully persuaded about the power of prayer, there is no crisis we cannot survive.

—FATHER ALBERT CYLWICKI

October 24

Do not neglect to do good and to share what you have, for such sacrifices are pleasing to God. —Hebrews 13:16

THE Holy Sacrifice of the Mass is the sublimest of prayers, the most significant of religious acts. Love for the Mass is the sign of a good Catholic. Yet there are many who seldom miss Mass but who nevertheless make poor witnesses for Christ in their workaday lives.

SOMETHING must be wrong with the participation of these people in the Mass. Participation which is sincere, devout, intelligent and full of faith should and does produce a discernible impact on the lives of the participants. The evidence of genuine participation in the Mass is manifested in a steady stream of acts of positive good — the constant effort to please God by working to make others happy.

HOW IS YOUR participation in the Mass? There is a simple way to check it. Can you scarcely wait to get out of the church after Mass so that you may do good to others?

—BISHOP ANDREW G. GRUTKA, Gary, Indiana

October 25

When you are in tribulation, and all these things come upon you in later years, you will return to the Lord your God and obey his voice, for the Lord your God is a merciful God; he will not fail you or destroy you or forget the covenant with your fathers which he swore to them. —Deuteronomy 4:30-31

I T does not take much effort to thank God for the serene brightness of an autumn day, the rusty gold of the falling leaves, the contentment of a happy home or the happy times we have shared with others.

OUR GRATITUDE is expansive when we reflect that God has sent His only-begotten Son to be Our Savior, that truth is revealed by Him in Christ, that we have the means of grace and salvation. But what of suffering? Should we not thank God for suffering also?

AS WE LOOK back on the signposts of pain, inconvenience and misfortune that we have encountered, we can see that perhaps these things have directed us toward God. Blessings in disguise we call them. But for the Christian who is aware of the Providence of God the disguise is thin.

—FATHER LEON MCKENZIE

October 26

Yet he bore the sin of many, and made intercession for the transgressors. —Isaiah 53:12

T HE last and chief requirement of friendship is the obligation to *self-sacrifice.* It is in this highest and final test that the Son of God has exalted the name of friendship to such a height of glory, that it should never be degraded to designate any of the selfish companionships of ignoble men.

"GREATER love hath no man than this, that a man lay down his life for his friends." And this is the love which Jesus has shown us. "Surely, He hath borne our griefs and carried our sorrows: He was wounded for our transgressions. He was bruised for our iniquities."

THERE IS not one of us, no matter how weak, who cannot claim this last and greatest sign of the friendship of Jesus, and say: "Who loved *me,* and gave Himself for *me!"*

SUCH is the friendship of Christ for us. This *is* what He means when He says, "I have called you friends."

—MSGR. CHARLES HUGO DOYLE

October 27

For you have need of endurance, so that you may do the will of God and receive what is promised. —Hebrews 10:36

WE are generally a very impatient people. In fact, sometimes so impatient that we can be described as wanting today's demands filled yesterday. We have become so accustomed to instant foods and drinks, instant telecommunications and other instantaneous things that we become impatient if everything doesn't come our way at our whim and fancy. Many people become impatient and even upbraid God when He doesn't give them an immediate affirmative answer to their prayers. They seem to think that their prayers should get them what they want when they want it.

OUR BLESSED MOTHER had to wait for an answer to her request at the wedding feast in Cana. St. Monica had to pray and pray and wait and wait for the conversion of her son Augustine; meanwhile, God favored her with unexpected blessings.

THE BEST time for our prayers to be granted is God's time.
—MSGR. RALPH G. KUTZ

October 28

God thunders wondrously with his voice; he does great things which we cannot comprehend. —Job 37:5

THE more we think of God's way with men, the clearer it becomes that He often uses very strange instruments to accomplish His greatest works. He employed the tongue-tied Moses to plead for the Jews before Pharaoh. He sent the fearful and fainthearted Jonah to preach to Nineveh. David, the adulterer and murderer, sang His sweetest psalms.

STRANGER still to our American ideas of efficiency and know-how was the sending of the Apostles, very unlikely candidates for greatness and most of them fishermen, on a mission such as this: "Go into all the world and preach the gospel to the whole creation" (Mark 16:15).

SIMON and Jude were two of the lesser known of that group of Apostles. After preaching the Gospel in the areas assigned to them, tradition has them being martyred together on the same day in Persia. Today St. Jude is frequently prayed to as a powerful intercessor for those in desperate straits.
—FATHER THOMAS M. BREW, S.J.

October 29

Let love be genuine; hate what is evil, hold fast to what is good; love one another with brotherly affection; outdo one another in showing honor. —Romans 12:9-10

THE way some people talk, it would seem that love of others was our century's great discovery. The careful student of Christianity knows that such is not the case. All the Christian centuries have had men and women spending themselves selflessly for suffering and neglected humanity. Every *Anno Domini* (Year of Our Lord) has had its zealous champions of the needy and downtrodden.

OUR CENTURY has discovered a new urgency to fulfill the precept of brotherly love. In a world that is dying for lack of love, we have this divine assignment to spread love where we find hatred. Our mission is to remind men of God's love for them and their world. Are we in earnest about carrying out our mission?

—FLORENCE WEDGE

October 30

Having gifts that differ according to the grace given to us, let us use them: if prophecy, in proportion to our faith; if service, in our serving; he who teaches, in his teaching; he who exhorts, in his exhortation; he who contributes, in liberality; he who gives aid, with zeal; he who does acts of mercy, with cheerfulness. —Romans 12:6-8

GIFTS, once received, are not meant to be returned. By receiving the grace to grow in the blessings of the gifts and fruits of the Holy Spirit, we enter into a covenant with God. It is a covenant of trust and love freely given by God. Once we join in union with Him and His promise, we take upon ourselves an awful burden. We are responsible for witnessing to the world a message which the world will most times refuse to hear.

BUT if we do our job honestly, the Lord has promised us the patience and the fortitude to use our knowledge wisely. He will give us as our defense, understanding, counsel, and mildness to carry the urgent and sometimes hard news of continence, modesty, chastity, long-suffering, and fear of the Lord.

OUR OWN lives will be marked by a faith grounded in piety, benignity, and goodness from which will flow out to others a charity, a joy, and a lasting peace.

—JAMES MICHAEL SULLIVAN

October 31

Woe to the faint heart, for it has no trust! Therefore it will not be sheltered. —Sirach 2:13

TODAY is Halloween, the evening before All Saints Day, a Holy Day become a holiday. Once it meant turning our thoughts toward our eventual destiny, the holy ones in Heaven and those in Purgatory. Fear turns piety to superstition to mockery and, at last, becomes the property of children. And so we have a jolly Santa Claus instead of the stark beauty of the Nativity and the Easter bunny instead of the glory of the risen Christ.

AS OCTOBER ends, the year goes into its old age. Winter, however it comes in your home, is at hand. Do not fear the going of the old year or its symbolic tinge that your life, too, will someday approach its end. There is a beauty to endings, as to beginnings. As a poet has said of death, it "is nothing strange and but a change in range. We only cease our having to believe." Go, then, in faith, wherever God's hand leads you.

—TERRY MARTIN

November 1

Greet every saint in Christ Jesus. The brethren who are with me greet you. All the saints greet you. . . . —Philippians 4:21-22

TODAY we celebrate the feast of All the Saints. So we wish you a happy feast day. We are the saints, as St. Paul pointed out a long time ago. We must never forget that there are saints in Heaven and must we also never forget that there are saints on earth.

WE ARE the saints on earth because we belong to the one, holy, catholic and apostolic Church. This is one of our greatest tributes, that we are the members of this Church militant, and, by the reason of our baptism, are destined to become members of the Church suffering (in Purgatory) and the Church triumphant (in Heaven).

FOR THIS REASON we rejoice today, on the feast of All Saints, for this is not only a commemoration of those who have gone before us, but also a celebration for all of us who are living for and looking for the world of the better things to come.

THIS FACT compels us to spend this month in meditating upon the Church.

—FATHER NICHOLAS M. ZIMMER

November 2

Out of the depths I cry to thee, O Lord! Lord, hear my voice! Let thy ears be attentive to the voice of my supplications!

—Psalms 130:1-2

THIS is another "All Saints" Day; for those in Purgatory are saints. You can show your lively belief in the "communion of saints" by helping the helpless saints, by offering Him who is Sanctity Incarnate sacrificed that humans might become Saints. Mass offered for those in Purgatory will manifest your *empathy* which is a form of genuine sanctity.

THE SOULS suffer, but with *joy*; for they know they have attained their goal — Sanctity; and that soon they will be with Him in whom they "lived, and moved, and had their being" — Jesus Christ. You, too, will suffer on earth. You should do it with *joy* — and thus make it part of your "Purgatory" as well as relieving those who are actually in Purgatory.

PURGATORY proves God's Mercy as well as His Justice — so does every slightest suffering you experience on earth. Offer it up!

—FATHER M. RAYMOND, O.C.S.O.

November 3

". . . I have seen the affliction of my people, because their cry has come to me." —I Samuel 9:16

S ISTER CARMEN SANDOVAL LIRA heard radio pleas for adults to take care of four children who had been abandoned in front of the Valparaiso city jail, where their mother was imprisoned. As the pleas continued through the day, she grew more anguished, until "it suddenly dawned on me that those calls were directed at me and nobody else would respond."

SHE TOOK CHARGE of the children, aged from nine months to five years. They formed the nucleus for a foundation for abandoned children until today there are over one hundred at Sister's Garden of Children in Chile.

IN THE 1600s St. Martin de Porres spent his days feeding and finding lodging for abandoned children in Peru. He is best honored by people like Sister Carmen who "listen" when appeals are being made and do something about them. Many people are never at home when God dials their number, or they do not answer His ring.

—ANNE TANSEY

November 4

". . . Blessed are the dead who die in the Lord . . . that they may rest from their labors, for their deeds follow them!" —Revelation 14:13

D URING the first two days of the month we commemorated the saints in Heaven and the souls in Purgatory. This includes all souls who lived and died before us in friendship with God. Those not included refused God's friendship and are lost forever in Hell.

THE LITURGICAL remembrance of these souls should help us realize two things: that someday we too will die; and that, if after death, we are not included in either of these commemorations . . . then our lives will have been tragic failures.

FAILURE is a relative term. A lack of wealth, accomplishment, power, social position tend to be indicators of worldly failure; but only the lack of God-life within a person is viewed as such by God.

MANY of the saints and souls in Purgatory would be classified as worldly failures, but according to God's standards they were wonderfully successful. Only by living in friendship with God are we assured of everlasting success.

—FATHER WILLIAM J. NEIDHART, C.S.C.

November 5

The mouth of the righteous utters wisdom, and his tongue speaks justice. —Psalms 37:30

ONE of the most gifted thinkers of our times was G. K. Chesterton, the English commentator. Chesterton, or GKC as he was affectionately called, had an incisive mind that could puncture the pomposity and cut through the phoniness of some of the popular critics, who told the fickle public what they wanted to hear. It is not a very honest thing to do, but it makes men rich.

AND ONE of the things these critics tell the people is that they do not need God. Yet as Chesterton pointed out it was precisely when man in petty pride cut himself loose from God — he got into all sorts of trouble. He drifted away from God, out of the safe harbor, out on the stormy sea, and poor man now seemingly has not the humility to turn back to God, our safe harbor and home.

CHESTERTON wrote: how foolish man can be and is when he deserts God. It ends only in the disaster of shipwreck.

—FATHER RAWLEY MYERS

November 6

He was praying in a certain place, and when he ceased, one of his disciples said to him, "Lord, teach us to pray. . . ." —Luke 11:1

WHAT does it mean to pray? We know that You have told us that we must pray, but sometimes it's hard. We forget. We're too busy. We're too tired.

YOU HAVE TOLD us to say "Our Father" when we pray. We can actually dare to call God, "Our Father." We can talk to Him as a father — as a person. Someone like our own father. Someone who understands us. Someone who cares for us, and someone who loves us.

THIS IS WHAT prayer is then: A talk with "Our Father." A conversation with a real person. It is a talk about ourselves; about what kind of day we've had, about our problems, and about our joys. God is a friend — the best friend we have — and He is more than willing to listen to us — anytime we want.

—MICHAEL DUNBAR

November 7

Wives, be subject to your husbands, as is fitting in the Lord. Husbands, love your wives, and do not be harsh with them.   —Colossians 3:18-19

WE so easily disillusion and disappoint each other. We fail to keep promises and are less than dependable. We hurt each other.

IF WE practice "the eight-letter — therapy" — I forgive and we forget, however, peace can happen again. If we do not have the capacity to forgive and forget we'll allow the cancer of dissatisfaction and revenge to grow and eat away at our happiness.

PAUL reminds us: Forgive one another as soon as a quarrel begins (Colossians 3:13). Do not stay angry all day. No more hateful feelings! Instead, be kind and forgive one another, as God has forgiven you (Ephesians 4).

CONTRARY to the *Love Story* theme: Love *is* saying you are sorry and forgiving someone who has hurt you. Don't keep the war going on in your body. Call a truce and make your mind a peaceful place to live.

—FATHER JOHN TORMEY

November 8

Let your manner of life be worthy of the gospel of Christ.
—Philippians 1:27

"OUR conversation," wrote St. Paul, "is in heaven." In today's language we would say, "Our country is heaven." St. Paul tells the Philippians, and us, that worldlings make a god of this world; of money, of their "ego," of sex. These, Paul points out, "are enemies of the Cross of Christ."

THESE DAYS of early November in the mind of the Church are glorious and brilliant harvest days, but also days of hard, cold fact. Sifting rains and cold harsh days are likewise here now that harvesting is over. On nights like these you can hear the eerie fluting of the wild geese as they pass high overhead, homing southward.

THE BLUNT question we must own up to is, are we honestly homesick for our true home? Do we genuinely admit our dependence, our creaturehood? If so, then we are humble, and God is first in our lives. Idolatry is the great blasphemy — to make our self, our pleasure, our financial rating a god.

—FATHER ROBERT L. WILKEN

November 9

"It is written, 'My house shall be called a house of prayer.' "
—Matthew 21:13

THE Basilica of St. John Lateran in Rome ranks even before St. Peter's as the central church of Catholicism: it is the cathedral of the Pope, Bishop of Rome. It was originally built by the Emperor Constantine in the three hundreds on the site where he himself was baptized by Pope Sylvester. At St. John Lateran important events connected with the Easter mysteries are celebrated: the first Sunday of Lent, Palm Sunday, Holy Thursday, the Easter Vigil.

WE MUST continue to come to Christ through every means He gives us: the successors to His Apostles, the sacraments they administer, the prayers we make.

LORD Jesus, let us appreciate all the gifts You give us which touch us with Your power.
—FATHER GARY LAUENSTEIN, C.SS.R.

November 10

How great are his signs, how mighty his wonders! —Daniel 4:3

THE leaves are gone, returned to their earth. Cool gray skies announce winter's nearness. Autumn's heart breaks forth upon us.

IT'S QUIET TIME. Time to wait, to pray and to hope. It is time to be alone with God's promise, and time to listen to the silence of His love. Nature will not die, just rest — peaceful, gentle rest. She will listen for her Lord, and you must listen also. You can almost smell it in the air these November mornings when the frosted dew quilts the earth with twinkled wonder. All of creation is listening ever so closely to the whisper of His voice. He is speaking in tender tones of love to the harvest fields, and the fields respond with plenty. From day's dawning to the closing of the light, He speaks to the heart of His people. You must listen in quiet hope to the roar of the secrets which He tells.

INCLINE the ear of your heart to the silent voice of His calling. Let His heart be yours. And let your heart be free.
—T. TIMOTHY DELANEY

November 11

". . . Among our captors he divides our fields." —Micah 2:4

O N this day in 1918, the warring powers declared an Armistice to World War I. (Little did they know that they would be facing a bigger war in two decades.) I was in an Egyptian hospital, then, after four years plus of front line hell and blood. The whole big hospital became a pandemonium. I stayed in my cot beholding all the shenanigans; and wondering. About what?

ABOUT ALL the immense multitudes of men and boys who would never go home: the Poor Souls already forgotten in all the bedlam. And more and more forgotten through all the years, even by those who should have remembered them best.

"MAN'S inhumanity to man" is well matched by man's ingratitude to God and man. What good are medals, citations, "patriotic" platitudes to the Poor Souls of battlefield dead? That there are so many neglected and forgotten souls is one reason for the Church's constant solicitude for all Poor Souls.

—FATHER WILLIAM J. BOAT

November 12

Hope deferred makes the heart sick, but a desire fulfilled is a tree of life. —Proverbs 13:12

N OTHING causes Our Lord so much sorrow and nothing is ultimately such a cause of harm to ourselves as our lack of confidence in His goodness and mercy. Our Faith and our Love are based on the goodness of God, since we believe in Him because He is so good and will not deceive us; and we love Him because he is so good and worthy of our love. But in practice our Hope is based rather on *our own* goodness, because it rises and falls, in step with the variation in the reports of our conscience. When we are good we trust God; when we are not so good, we feel that we cannot have the same confidence.

THIS IS COMPLETELY wrong. We should hope in God because *He* is infinitely good and merciful. Our own defects should not lessen our hopes in His goodness, since He uses them to glorify His mercy. St. Paul gloried in his infirmities; we should do the same, being certain that the grace of God — and His goodness — is sufficient for us: for our sufficiency is from God.

—FATHER EUGENE BOYLAN, O.C.S.O.

November 13

For the word of the cross is folly to those who are perishing, but to us who are being saved it is the power of God. —1 Corinthians 1:18

IN his book, *Death of Jesus,* Leonard Johnston said that the Cross should be no bitter reminder to a Christian. Rather than accept it with tears and lamentations we should look upon it as a permanent Metanoia, an acknowledgment of our separation from God but also a proclamation of our will to return to Him.

THIS ATTITUDE is pointed up by a story told about Saint Frances Xavier Cabrini. She was taking a new band of recruits from her convent in Italy to work in the hospitals, orphanages and homes of charity which she had established in the United States.

THE RELATIVES of one young nun accompanied her to the pier, weeping, wailing and creating quite a scene. The departing Sister was just as emotional. "Go back to the convent," Mother Cabrini commanded, "God would not ask that much sacrifice from anyone."

—ANNE TANSEY

November 14

Nation shall not lift up sword against nation, neither shall they learn war any more. —Micah 4:3

THOMAS MORE in his classic book *Utopia* tells us that war is one of man's greatest enemies. This ancient "evil thing is the foe of the only way of life worth living, of the only kind of advancement worth striving for." As Pope Paul VI cried out at the United Nations in 1965, "No more war — war never again."

JESUS said, "Blessed are the peacemakers." Yes, blessed are those who promote peace and brotherhood among men. And this is not just for our Secretary of State, but for everyone in every neighborhood.

WHEREVER there is conflict, whoever helps to put an end to it, in a home, in a block of homes, in a community, in a nation or among nations — that person is a peacemaker. And blessed is such an individual.

—MARK GRACE

November 15

Blessed is the man who meditates on wisdom and who reasons intelligently. —Sirach 14:20

D OCTOR Albert would not go along with the crowd at Cologne University who put Thomas Aquinas down for a big oaf and lummox. Just because this quiet, retiring student, Thomas, looked hulking and seemed less the hale mixer and punster, St. Albert would not snub or cut him off as boorish. Others did.

GREAT MEN and saints can be made or can be stunted for life by unfeeling, unwise, and therefore uncharitable, remarks and attitudes. All of us are so much the creation of our environment — plus divine grace. Sly digs, complete insensitivity to the feelings of others have warped untold millions.

HUMBLE PEOPLE like Dr. Albert had genuine interest and sympathy for backward and awkward souls. Sensing the need these backward-seeming people had for kindness and encouragement, these saints touched others only to uplift and to draw out. Again it is from the humble, from those who feel strongly their need of God and of others, that one finds the Christian gentleman.

—FATHER ROBERT L. WILKEN

November 16

". . . Give light to those who sit in darkness and in the shadow of death, to guide our feet into the way of peace." —Luke 1:79

I N the Mass honoring St. Gertrude Our Lord warns us, "Watch . . . you know neither the day nor the hour." One secret of the saints is that they lived always ready to die. The time meant little to them because they were in constant friendship with God.

IN THE PARABLE of the ten virgins we can imagine how dejected the five foolish ones were when they considered their stupidity. But in real life the person who gambles with God's friendship, the person who deliberately rejects it for something else . . . such a person is a fool.

GOD ALONE knows how many souls have uttered the cry after death, "Lord, Lord, open to us," only to hear the reply, "Of a truth I tell you, I do not know you."

WE MUST be like the five wise virgins: always ready for the Bridegroom. It isn't difficult . . . not when you really love Him.

—FATHER WILLIAM J. NEIDHART, C.S.C.

November 17

Our heart has not turned back, nor have our steps departed from thy way. . . . —Psalms 44:18

LIFE is a divine romance. Thus did God plan it from the beginning. Thus has God restored it after the Fall. But we must make it such; for love without liberty is not love at all. God loves us.

ELIZABETH OF HUNGARY serves as a splendid model. She knew human love, almost perfect human romance. Espoused at the age of four, she was married at fourteen. Ten years later she was dead but only after living in love for six years, giving birth to three children out of love, then spending four years of widowhood in love with God.

WIDOW, it is said, is a lonely word — just how lonely only widows know. Yet, when a widow loves God as Elizabeth did she can say: "Lord, You know I loved my husband more than anything in this world . . . but as it has pleased You to call him to Yourself, I am resigned to Your will; and if by saying one *Our Father* I could recall him to life against Your will, I would not say it."

—FATHER M. RAYMOND, O.C.S.O.

November 18

"It is written, 'Man shall not live by bread alone, but by every word that proceeds from the mouth of God.'" —Matthew 4:4

OLIVE, a huge Cistercian monastery of the tenth century, is near Danzig. In 1217, famine existed in the country near Gdenek. The Cistercian monks baked bread daily and gave it to the poor.

ONE DAY, a man took his share and returned to ask for more. The Brother asked: "Have you had your share?" Quickly he lied: "No! This is the first I am getting!" The Brother gave him another loaf and the man returned to Danzig. On his way, he met a woman carrying a sleeping child. "Will you give me some bread?" she pleaded. "My child is hungry." "I have no bread," he lied nervously. "B—but aren't you hiding a loaf beneath your cloak?" "Oh, no! It's — it's not bread. It's, it's a stone," he lied again.

"LET IT be so," she sighed and moved on. Soon, the loaf, beneath his cloak, grew heavy. Looking at it, he saw a huge stone. Running back to the monastery, he confessed his sin and left the stone there as a warning to other weak souls.

—MARIE LAYNE

November 19

And whatever you do, in word or deed, do everything in the name of the Lord Jesus, giving thanks to God the Father through him.

—Colossians 3:17

THERE were two commandments of God which summed up the Old Testament Law and were approved by Christ. The first bade us to love God, and the second to love our neighbor — as ourself. The evening before He died, Our Lord modified the terms of the second one. Giving a new commandment, He told us to love one another "as I have loved you."

HE LAID DOWN fraternal charity as the characteristic mark by which Christians should be recognized. And in His revelation of the last judgment, He chose charity as the ultimate test. In doing so, He enunciated the principle that governs all our relations with one another. "Whatsoever you do to the least of these you do it to Me."

FOR WEAL OR WOE, everything that we do to a neighbor is done to Christ. If we hurt them, we hurt Christ; if we help them, we help Christ. That is the terrible responsibility, and at the same time, the wonderful privilege of being a Christian.

—FATHER EUGENE BOYLAN, O.C.S.O.

November 20

"Let the children come to me, do not hinder them; for to such belongs the kingdom of God. Truly, I say to you, whoever does not receive the kingdom of God like a child shall not enter it." —Mark 10:14-15

BE still, my friend, and listen to the voice of the children. Hear the words they speak and the love of which they tell in their playing out of the gentleness of Jesus. Listen to the children and become young once more.

SCRIPTURE exhorts us to be like the children, for such is the kingdom of God. "Let the children come to me," He said. And they did and were happy. Unless you become as children there shall be no entrance to His Kingdom. So we must listen to the children and hear what they say. They speak of gentleness and joy. Be gentle with yourself, and for others be a cause of joy. They show us laughter and the freedom of play. You must learn and develop a sense of the humor of life, and be able to laugh at yourself and with the world. Also, take some time to play, to relax, and to be alone with God. Prayer and play are so closely connected that it is hardly possible to have one, truly, without the other.

—T. TIMOTHY DELANEY

November 21

I will cause your name to be celebrated in all generations; therefore the peoples will praise you for ever and ever. —Psalms 45:17

THE VIRGIN MARY was presented by her holy parents to God in the temple at Jerusalem. By this ceremony she was dedicated to God while still an infant.

SHE WAS "from the first clothed in sanctity." And because she was all her life so near to God, we turn to her for help. It is the most natural thing in the world, for she is our Mother and the person closest to Christ. If men sought out the Apostles to speak for them to Christ, how much more so should we go to His Mother.

MARY is our chief intercessor with her Son. She is grace and smiling light. She is not like earthly beauty but bright and pure like the morning star.

—FATHER RAWLEY MYERS

November 22

And David and all Israel were making merry before God with all their might, with song and lyres and harps and tambourines and cymbals and trumpets. —1 Chronicles 13:8

ALL THAT we know officially of St. Cecilia is that she was a martyr under the Roman Emperor Alexander Severus around 230 A.D. Yet, legends of her have enriched and instructed Christendom down through the ages. She is considered the patroness of musicians because, legend says, her husband happened in upon her on their wedding night while she was at prayer and he found her prayers accompanied by the singing of Angels.

ACCORDING to the legend, this led to the conversion of her husband, his brother also, their arrest and the conversion of the jailer, and finally martyrdom.

IF WE HAD enough faith, our way of life would prove a great contribution to the lives of others, no matter how insignificant it may seem to us.

BLESS us in this, Jesus.

—FATHER GARY LAUENSTEIN, C.SS.R.

November 23

Thou visitest the earth and waterest it, thou greatly enrichest it; . . .
Thou crownest the year with thy bounty; the tracks of thy chariot drip
with fatness. —Psalms 65:9, 11

L OVE never gives up. On Thanksgiving Day, it is truly
meaningful to remember and be indebted for those loves in our
lives that have not given up. We offer thanks for the loves we struggle
to understand better each day.

A LOVE that is really meant to be never gives up. In the worst
of times, there is a flickering light, no matter how dim. There is
something to be saved. There is something that can live again.

THAT IS why hoping is such an important part of loving. It is
not a blind or naive kind of hoping. Our love has known much pain
— pain that cannot be erased. But it is a pain that can be built upon:
Hope tells us that tomorrow can be better than yesterday if we have
the courage to act on the things we know need correcting.

—JAMES MICHAEL SULLIVAN

November 24

Blessed are those whose way is blameless, who walk in the law of the
Lord! —Psalms 119:1

T HERE are many links between the message of salvation and
human culture. For God, revealing himself to His people to the
extent of a full manifestation of himself in His Incarnate Son, has
spoken according to the culture proper to different ages.

LIVING IN VARIOUS circumstances during the course of
time, the Church, too, has used in her preaching the discoveries of
different cultures to spread and explain the message of Christ to all
nations, to probe it and more deeply understand it, and to give it
better expression in liturgical celebrations and in the life of the
diversified community of the faithful.

BUT AT THE SAME time, the Church, sent to all peoples of
every time and place, is not bound exclusively and indissolubly to
any race or nation, nor to any particular way of life or any customary
pattern of living, ancient or recent. Faithful to her own tradition and
conscious of her universal mission, she can enter into all modes of
life.

—FATHER NICHOLAS M. ZIMMER

November 25

"The kingdom of the world has become the kingdom of our Lord and of his Christ, and he shall reign for ever and ever." —Revelation 11:15

INSTITUTING the feast of Christ the King, Pope Pius XI continually emphasized that the peace of Christ would come to mankind only when the Kingship of Christ was universally recognized.

OFTEN, the forces of anti-Christ have grown stronger and extended the number of nations and peoples. Many have not yet grasped the fundamental idea that there is one alternative to the forces of anti-God: the acceptance of Christ the King. Reviewing Christ's Kingship, let us turn our hearts and prayers to Christ. Remind Him you will always surrender to His will.

ACCEPT CHRIST, each day, as King to reign over your life. Others about you will feel your example and influence. Christ has a right to ardent love from mankind. He has a right to expect willing service from those who call themselves Christians.

—MARIE LAYNE

November 26

"Gather to me my faithful ones, who made a covenant with me by sacrifice!" —Psalms 50:5

THE mighty Mass! What would the Poor Souls do without it? What would we do without it?

THIS POOR writer knows perfectly well that the Mass brought him unscathed through the awful carnage of the 1915 Dardanelles campaign (casualties ninety per cent) and through many other campaigns and dangers, temporal and spiritual, through 1914-19. (He was a front line noncom.)

IN the midst of the slaughtered thousands I stood erect—and wondered. I did not realize then that the Mass was holding me up.

LONG after the war I found out that two Masses had been offered for me every week throughout the conflict. One given by a poor but valiant mother, the other by a wonderful Ursuline Sister.

THE MASS reaches a long way, and, as that Irish mother used to say, "The Lord sends far off." Maybe the Mass pulled me through to write for the Poor Souls!

—FATHER WILLIAM J. BOAT

November 27

For it is the God who said, "Let light shine out of darkness," who has shown in our hearts to give the light of knowledge of the glory of God in the face of Christ. —2 Corinthians 4:6

IN a sense November resembles interior religion. The real essence becomes apparent as passing days strip us of things which have obscured our pure vision of God. The harvest of September kept us in alien fields. The beauty of October foliage led us down unfamiliar trails in our search for the exotic in nature's color and tone.

THE WINDS of November have swept from the trees the fleeting beauty which dazzled our eyes. Snow has covered familiar terrain. As winter progresses sun is sparse, days go earlier into darkness.

WITH EXTERNAL delights gone, there is no place to go but into ourselves — and there is God, waiting for us, patiently. He is not screened behind scenes and events. There is no corner to turn to avoid Him. Without even our fig leaves we cannot avoid His questioning eyes.

—ANNE TANSEY

November 28

Working together with him, then, we entreat you not to accept the grace of God in vain. For he says, "At the acceptable time I have listened to you, and helped you on the day of salvation."
—2 Corinthians 6:1-2

IT is very easy for us to take pride in our own work. We can become very selfish and very protective of our own little projects. We resent people telling us what to do or others taking over.

PAUL was aware of this, and he warned against it. The work we are to do is Christ's work. It is for His glory not our own, Christ's Church belongs to Him and not to us.

WE DO the groundwork, the planting and the watering of the faith, and it's all very important. But we do not give the growth. Only God can do that.

HELP US Lord to remember that we are working for You. Everything we do belongs to You and is not our own private little possession.

—MICHAEL DUNBAR

November 29

Do not love the world or the things of the world. If any one loves the world, love for the Father is not in him. For all that is in the world, the lust of the flesh and the lust of the eyes and the pride of life, is not of the Father but is of the world. —1 John 2:15-16

WE all want to be happy in life. But self-seeking, self-loving is not the way. It is rather the direct antithesis of real living. The moment a person starts to become unselfish, he finds himself in touch with real life, and with God.

THE PERSON in selfishness who exploits others will never be happy. He may be rich, but never happy. Those, for example, who make a lot of money selling sex in one form or another are headed for real misery. The Christ-follower, on the other hand, seeks to help others grow in soul and not destroy them.

THE CHRISTIAN holds up ideals which men need to survive spiritually and enjoy happiness in this life.

—MARK GRACE

November 30

He first found his brother Simon, and said to him, "We have found the Messiah" (which means Christ). —John 1:41

HOW fitting it is to round off this month dedicated to your own "communing with the saints" by celebrating the feast of that Apostle who first found Jesus — St. Andrew.

WHEN JOHN the Baptist pointed to Jesus Christ and said: "Behold the Lamb of God," this young fisherman immediately set out to follow Christ. It was Andrew who called his brother, Simon, to Christ, thus leading the Rock to Him who would build His Church thereon.

WHAT A MODEL for us grasping humans! He was the first to find Christ, the first to follow Christ, the first to recognize Christ as Messiah. Yet, after all these "firsts," where do we find Andrew? — Outside the "inner circle." But no envy in his heart. He had found Christ. Nothing else mattered.

THE GREATEST act in the world today will be the Holy Sacrifice of Mass. You can assist at that! The greatest happening in the world today will be the coming of Christ in Holy Communion to any soul. You can be an actor in that greatest of all happenings.

—FATHER M. RAYMOND, O.C.S.O.

December 1

Be patient, therefore, brethren until the coming of the Lord.
—James 5:7

A DVENT begins the Church's new year of grace. Advent invites us to begin anew our new journey in the grace of Christ. For that reason, spiritual writers tell us that the spiritual life is a series of new beginnings.

ADVENT invites us to a period of meditation, of examination. It is our time of preparing for the coming of Christ. But Christ comes in many ways. He will come, to be sure, on Christmas morn. But He will also come whenever the grace of God is stirred up in our hearts. For this reason Advent should be a time of more frequent and fervent meditation and examination. Through such means we will be more concerned with spiritual than temporal matters. In such a way the grace of God will be able to work more effectively in our souls.

ADVENT is our time of spiritual re-birth. By opening the eyes of our soul through prayer and meditation we will be better able to see the Birth of Christ on Christmas morn.
—FATHER VINCENT A. YZERMANS

December 2

One man gives freely, yet grows all the richer; another withholds what he should give, and only suffers want. —Proverbs 11:24

H OW many shopping days until Christmas? That thought may be a trifle agitating this soon after Thanksgiving, but the highpoint in the year's holidays is closer than we think. We can begin now to prepare the traditional Christmas check-list.

THERE IS no need for shuddering anxiety; anticipation is more than half the fun. For most of us, happiness is having something — or someone — to look forward to. A child's sense of expectancy is a sure guarantee of a joyous holiday season.

CHRISTMAS is a feast of Faith, as well as an occasion for a visit from Santa. We stand on tiptoe for the coming of the inner gift of Christmas Faith: a sharpened awareness of the reality of Christ in our life of grace. Grace is not a rigid "state." This life we share in Christ is dynamic, moving, powerful. Christmas can teach us this.
—MSGR. FRANCIS TOURNIER

December 3

Some were tortured, refusing to accept release, that they might rise again to a better life. Others suffered mocking and scourging, and even chains and imprisonment. —Hebrews 11:35-36

THE great colossus of China, held in the iron grip of atheistic Communism, has threatened the peace of the world.

IT WAS the dream of St. Francis Xavier that China might be converted to Christianity. He brought Christ to the people of India and Japan and he was ready to carry his missionary efforts to China when he died, a young man of only 46. Saint Pius X named this great Jesuit the patron of the missionary efforts of the Church.

TODAY as you go to Mass in freedom, as you openly proclaim your faith, join the saints in Heaven with your prayer for those in prisons, for those who must worship in secret, in the country St. Francis dreamed would one day be Christian. The blood of martyrs will help save China.

—DALE FRANCIS

December 4

Once you were darkness, but now you are light in the Lord. . . .
—Ephesians 5:8

HERE'S a recipe for a do-it-yourself kit. One that can bring us nearer the Christmas crib.

IT'S CALLED the Advent Wreath, and it will help get your home in the proper spirit of the season. You'll need a round frame of wire, covering it with branches of evergreen or fir. The sprigs symbolize our hope in the redemption.

FOUR CANDLES are tied to the frame, and each represents a thousand years. Thus: the four thousand years that the chosen people waited for Christ — and the four weeks of Advent. The flame represents the Light of the world. With each Sunday, another candle is lit, indicating the closer approach of the Savior.

A PURPLE RIBBON is added, for Advent is a season of prayer and penance.

SEEING the Wreath (which makes a lovely centerpiece) will remind all that Christmas doesn't merely consist of a reindeer with a shiny nose, toys, goodies or ten-year-old Scotch. . . . It is a serious time of thought and penance.

—FATHER PETER V. ROGERS, O.M.I.

December 5

He came for testimony, to bear witness to the light, that all might believe through him. He was not the light, but came to bear witness to the light. —John 1:7-8

S T. JOHN THE BAPTIST, with Our Lady, is the great figure of Advent. His voice cries through the wilderness of secular festivity: Repent! The Lord is coming! Face up to reality. It's no use saying, "I'm OK, I'm baptized." The Lord does not judge by appearances or hearsay. He judges by the reality of a Christian life, the fruits of the harvest. Wheat is kept. Chaff is burnt. But both come from the same stem.

WE LOOK forward to Christmas, sincerely seeking to recapture the simplicity and goodness of children. But in this cynical day and age even children learn to calculate Christmas by the gifts it yields.

SOMEHOW, in this wilderness, we must build a solid, straight freeway for Christ who is bringing His Spirit of *real* peace . . . not the tinsel wishes of commercial carols and cards.

PEACE and prosperity will come when "the whole country is filled with the knowledge of Yahweh, as waters swell the sea."

—ANNE O'NEILL

December 6

With every gift show a cheerful face. . . . —Sirach 35:9

M ILLIONS of children, young and old, are familiar with jolly old St. Nick but few of them know anything about the original St. Nicholas and not much about the spirit of Christian giving which he symbolizes.

WE LIVE AS WE GIVE. This is one way of expressing the whole message of the Gospel. The Dead Sea is dead because it has no outlet; it receives but does not give. Hence there is no current of fresh water throughout.

THIS CAN BE TRUE OF LIFE. A completely self-centered, self-contained, self-satisfied person would make his life a fool's paradise on earth, but it would really be a prison with the high wall and when he died he would turn his face to the wall. With no circuit maintained between him and God, there would be no real communication, no real contact, no light and no life. Unless we give we do not live in the full sense of the word.

—BISHOP LEO A. PURSLEY, Fort Wayne-South Bend, Indiana

December 7

Some went down to the sea in ships. ... —Psalms 107:23

ONE of the first American Catholic Chaplains to be lost in the Second World War was the Rev. Aloysius H. Schmidt of the Archdiocese of Dubuque. Father Schmidt died a heroic death aboard the USS Oklahoma, during the bombing of Pearl Harbor on December 7, 1941.

AS THE Oklahoma sank Father Schmidt, who had done everything he could to help the other sailors to be saved, was trapped in one of the cabins. He was last seen looking from the porthole as he waved with his hand in which he held the Rosary. In a few moments the waves had swallowed him and thus he met his God. His thoughts must have been directed to Our Lady as he solved the mystery of life.

IF WE PRAY the Rosary and love the Rosary in life, we may confidently trust that we shall be blessed by Our Lady's presence at the hour of our death.

—BISHOP JOHN J. CARBERRY, Lafayette-in-Indiana

December 8

"Hail, full of grace, the Lord is with you!" —Luke 1:28

TODAY is the Feast of the Immaculate Conception, commemorating Mary's preservation, alone among humans, from original sin. Most perceptive people believe in original sin even though they may call it something else. It is unfortunately and clearly easier to behave badly than well.

TODAY, rather than considering Mary's humanity, let us consider how she is *not* like us. Let our symbol be the moon.

OUR SOURCE of life and light on earth is the sun, yet we can never look at it directly. To do so blinds us permanently. The moon gives light only by reflecting the light of the sun. The moon, scientists theorize, was once part of the earth. Although astronauts have walked there now, she, unchanged, fills our nights with beauty, engages our imagination, consoles the lonely by her peace. She does not touch the earth, but she pulls our oceans' tides and the flow of our own blood. She sends into our dark nights the reflected light of another day.

—TERRY MARTIN

December 9

My foot has held fast to his steps; I have kept his way and have not turned aside.   —Job 23:11

O N December 7, 374, a man named Ambrose was ordained Bishop of Milan (Italy). Only a few days before he had been a pagan. In fact, he had been the civil governor of the province.

BUT THE PEOPLE were so impressed with his abilities to settle arguments, they demanded his baptism and ordination as bishop. Ambrose fulfilled his charge well, even under civil threat.

WHEN AMBROSE, as Bishop of Milan, refused to give in to the unjust demands over Church property which the emperor was making, the bishop took refuge in his basilica. There, surrounded on the inside by his people eager to protect him, and surrounded outside the church by the emperor's soldiers commanded to arrest him, the bishop began composing hymns: an example of his tireless and unconquerable spirit.

LORD JESUS, in you we have our strength.
                              —FATHER GARY LAUENSTEIN, C.SS.R.

December 10

Offer right sacrifices, and put your trust in the Lord.   —Psalms 4:5

T HESE weeks before Christmas find us busy cleaning, decorating, baking, shopping — just all full of gladness and peace.

FOR SOME it may be a peaceful preparation. But for the rest of us, it's hectic! The atmosphere is tense and close to explosive. There's so much you want to do. The cookies baked for the holidays are already gone, including the hidden ones. The recently cleaned house looks like a tornado hit it in spite of all your yelling "Wipe your feet!" "Pick up your things!" The money saved for that special gift went when the water heater gasped its last. Your nerves are frayed. You're out-of-sorts. You'll be glad when Christmas is over! You're sure not preparing the way for the Lord. The devil got in there somehow.

MAKE THIS ADVENT different. Cut down on your preparations if they make you grouchy and impatient. Set a goal for yourself. Relax with your family and let them help with the preparations. Stress the spiritual side. Really prepare the way for the Lord with a calm, joyful spirit.

                              —MUJANA DARIAN

December 11

O let the evil of the wicked come to an end, but establish thou the righteous, thou who triest the minds and hearts, thou righteous God. —Psalms 7:9

S T. DAMASUS. The Spaniard Damasus was Pope from 366 to 384. During his reign he had to contend with an anti-pope at Rome, schism at Antioch, Constantinople, and Sardinia, and Arian heresy over the whole Empire. St. Jerome, whom he commissioned to prepare the Vulgate translation of the Bible, calls him "an incomparable person, learned in the Scriptures, a virgin doctor of the virgin Church, who loved chastity and heard its praise with pleasure."

POPE DAMASUS had great veneration for the Christian martyrs, wrote many of the epitaphs for their tombs, and, out of humility, would not allow himself to be buried among his martyred predecessors.

ST. DAMASUS is buried in the Roman church at St. Laurence in Damaso, which he himself built. Today we ask him to inspire in us a love of reading the Sacred Scriptures. He ordered that the reading of each psalm be closed with the "Glory be to the Father. . . ."

—MSGR. THOMAS J. TOBIN

December 12

My eyes will be open and my ears attentive to the prayer that is made in this place. —2 Chronicles 7:15

I N early December, 1531, Juan Diego, a poor simple Indian only one generation removed from paganism, was traveling the barren plains on a three-day hike to Mass in Mexico City. Suddenly the Blessed Mother appeared to him and asked that a shrine be built on the spot in her honor. Later to convince the skeptical bishop, she had Juan gather roses, rare in the wintertime, into his rough blanket. When the bishop opened the blanket, all saw the miraculous image of Mary, the same image that still hangs in the great Basilica of Guadalupe near Mexico City.

MARY WAS NAMED Patroness of all Spanish America, including vast sections of our own southwest. To Juan Diego she was his personal Patroness, and the poor humble Indian, enriched by the attention of Mary, must have pondered: Why does she choose me, why does she love me?

—FATHER JOSEPH A. VAUGHAN, S.J.

December 13

In many-colored robes she is led to the king, with her virgin companions, her escort, in her train. —Psalms 45:14

S T. LUCY, a virgin and martyr, died about 304, betrayed by a pagan whom she refused to marry. She is invoked against blindness probably because her name is similar to the Latin *lucis* meaning "of light." An attempt to set her afire failed and she was slain by a sword.

ON HER FEAST we ask for light that we may know God's way. We also ask for guidance should we become physically blind as well as for protection from a spiritual loss of vision. Today we are tempted on all sides by the slogans of the materialists who say: "Be practical; don't be fooled by the promise of 'pie in the sky.' Get down to earth; take advantage of today, here and now. You won't live forever."

ST. LUCY should be invoked to help us keep our eyes on the important goals of life so that we may not be distracted by evil temptations. She can guide us on the road to eternal success.
—FATHER JOHN M. MARTIN, M.M.

December 14

. . . When his mother Mary had been betrothed to Joseph, before they came together she was found to be with child of the Holy Spirit.
—Matthew 1:18

M ARY conceived the God-Man by the power of the Holy Spirit. Mary's love exceeds the comprehension of both men and Angels combined.

WHAT A LIFE of joyful intimacy Jesus and Mary had for nine months! Man could never have thought of it. It is beyond man's imagination. It is more of a wonder than the mystery it is.

MARY was meant to be the "mold" of not only the Son of God but also of all the sons of God! By the power of the Holy Spirit, Mary shapes and forms us until we give birth to Christ in our souls. Nothing delights her more. So much is this true that when we say "Mary," she says "Jesus."
—FATHER BRUCE RISKI, O.F.M., Cap.

December 15

Rejoice in the Lord always; again I will say, Rejoice.
—Philippians 4:4

IT is during Advent that I recall that You, my God, came to us in a very special, yet very ordinary, way. You became like us in all things, except sin. In this way You revealed yourself to us as a "helping God," one who holds us "by the right hand."

HELP ME believe that my sorrow is Your sorrow, my joy Your joy.

YOU ARE constantly there, yet how often I forget this. Every time You try to take me by the hand I run away as if You were a stranger.

HELP ME this Advent to want You to come into my life a little more.

—PHILIP J. BRIGANTI

December 16

How often would I have gathered your children together as a hen gathers her brood under her wings, and you would not.
—Matthew 23:37

WE raised chickens when I was a little girl and one of my happier childhood memories is of taking the baby chicks from the hatchery boxes and starting them out in the brooder house. Each yellow ball of fluff had to be lifted out of the cardboard carton and encouraged to take its first sip of water and to peck at the feed scattered on newspapers.

BESIDES the commercial chickens from the hatchery we usually had a brood of little banty chicks running around with their mother hen. One of the most endearing analogies in the Bible has always seemed to me to be Christ's lament, "How often would I have gathered your children together, as a hen gathers her young under her wings and you would not!"

WHEN we are daunted by the challenges of a world too big for us it is good to remember that the love of God encompasses us as the soft, warm wings of the mother hen.

—TERRY MARTIN

December 17

Behold, a young woman shall conceive and bear a son and shall call his name Immanuel.   —Isaiah 7:14

ADVENT was a thoughtful time for Mary and Joseph. Why had they been chosen for the greatest event in human history? They were not rich, influential, nor highly educated. By what reasoning had God considered *them* "qualified" to do such great work?

MARY was not only to give birth to the Son of God, but to rear Him, clothe and feed Him, teach and guide Him. Being filled with the Holy Spirit she remained "herself." God had chosen her as she was, therefore she should remain what she was and this she did. Joseph remained a carpenter and taught the trade to Jesus.

GOD CHOSE each one of us to be what we are, to do what we are doing, no matter what our work may be. The important thing is how well we do it, how much we allow ourselves to be guided by God.

—ANNE TANSEY

December 18

Mary said, "My soul magnifies the Lord, and my spirit rejoices in God my Savior. . . ."   —Luke 1:46-47

MARY'S Canticle is a song of affirmation. Mary wholly accepts herself for who and what she is. Honestly and happily she admits to being humble. Boldly but truthfully she announces an "unthinkable" prophecy: "All ages shall call me blessed!" As the crowds said of Christ: "No man has ever spoken as this man!" so too, can it be said: "No woman has ever spoken as this woman!"

BEING humble, Mary acknowledges, in the same breath, the source of her uniqueness and holiness: "God has done great things for me." She realizes God "raises the lowly to high places." Her lowliness has won her God's favor.

TO A FAR lesser degree can the affirming words of Mary be re-echoed by us. If we become holy, we will be held in blessed memory. If we accept who and what we are, God will affirm us by His mighty graces. We will sing a Canticle proclaiming God's greatness.

—FATHER BRUCE RISKI, O.F.M.,Cap.

December 19

Have no anxiety about anything, but in everything by prayer and supplication with thanksgiving let your requests be made known to God. —Philippians 4:6

GRANT me the grace today, Lord, to accept Your word and to place my trust in You as Your Blessed Mother did. Let her be a model for me as a person who was willing to devote her whole life to serving Your Father. She accepted Your word and became Your mother.

I AM NOT FACED with such an awesome responsibility, yet I often fail, fail miserably in even small things.

I AM WEAK: I am afraid. I often find it hard to believe in You. Lord, help me today to remember the example of Your mother, to know amid the confusion of everyday life that You are truly with me, that Your Kingdom is at hand.

—ROBERT MEEHAN

December 20

". . . And this will be a sign for you: you will find a babe wrapped in swaddling cloths and lying in a manger." —Luke 2:12

CRIBS are going up all over Christendom today; they seem essential to Christmas joy. Gazing on our favorite crib arrangements at the parish church or at home, we should not ignore the silent presence of St. Joseph. We may be tempted to treat him as simply part of the Christmas pageantry, a lifeless plaster statue. But Joseph was a man, a "just man" the Scripture says, and his very real trials would have fractured lesser strength.

WHEN WE are bewildered over the direction we should take, especially when the demands of family responsibility seem to crowd out all sense and peace, then we can turn to Joseph, strong and patient and good.

JOSEPH is the foster-father of our love for God. Just as he struggled to understand the mission entrusted to him, so he will guide us and guard us in our search for peace that lasts.

—MSGR. FRANCIS TOURNIER

December 21

"For you shall go out in joy, and be led forth in peace; the mountains and hills before you shall break forth into singing, and all the trees of the field shall clap their hands. . . ." —Isaiah 55:12

L ISTEN to the joyful announcement of Isaiah our preacher in Advent:

"SO MANY athirst; who will not come to the water? So many destitute; who will come and get him food, get wine and milk free, no price to be paid? What, always spending, and no bread to eat, always toiling, and never a full belly? Do but listen, here you shall find content; here are dainties shall ravish your hearts. To my summons give heed and hearing; so your spirits shall revive; a fresh covenant awaits you, this time eternal; gracious promise of mine to David shall be ratified now. Before all the world my witness thou, a prince and a ruler among the nations! Summons of thine shall go out to a nation thou never knewest; peoples that never heard of thee shall hasten to thy call; such the glory thy God, the Holy One of Israel, has bestowed on thee. To the Lord betake you, while he may yet be found; cry out, while he is close at hand to hear. Leave rebel his ill-doing, sinner his guilty thoughts and come back to the Lord . . . so rich in pardon."

—MSGR. THOMAS J. TOBIN

December 22

Do not be conformed to this world but be transformed by the renewal of your mind, that you may prove what is the will of God, what is good and acceptable and perfect. —Romans 12:2

A MERICA loves the success story, the hero rising from rags to riches. The life of Mother Cabrini is a modern, American success story.

BUT HER STORY is in its own rare category. Sanctity and success mingled in equal measure. While the former newsboy was building his financial empire, the Italian immigrant girl was building her own kind of kingdom over wide areas of the western world.

SHE IS A STRIKING example of the truth of Francis Thompson's terse phrase: "Holiness energizes." It is love in action. We need not be concerned here with the superiority of the contemplative over the active life. There is much of both in each. Nobody ever became a Saint by neglecting to pray.

—BISHOP LEO A. PURSLEY, Fort Wayne-South Bend, Indiana

December 23

The Lord is near to all who call upon him, to all who call upon him in truth. —Psalms 145:18

CHRISTMAS wishes can ring hollow when we read the newspapers and watch the news of the world today, like any other day. Where is all this peace and happiness Christianity talks about? It's there. Today we see it lying in a manger, unrecognized by most. Here is peace of *heart*, the happiness that comes from seeking God first and His justice.

UNCONSTRAINED by human values and conceited self-confidence, we kneel to adore the child in the manger. We believe; we trust. We ask Him to shine through us, offering our own lives and our own families to give the Light of eternal life full scope in the world. For Christ is born again in these days in *us*. Let's not narrow the horizon of this Light that floods creation today.

—ANNE O'NEILL

December 24

You also be patient. Establish your hearts, for the coming of the Lord is at hand. —James 5:8

CHRISTMAS Eve — the evening of the weary travelers who found no room. We who have shelter on this day should remember the homeless tonight.

CONSIDER the *barrianos* of Latin America . . . the refugees of Asia . . . the unemployed who cannot find rent money . . . the drifters on our city streets.

CONSIDER, too, those who have found no room in any other human heart. How many of the elderly, the deformed, the outcasts of society "are making friends with death" this very evening because they have no human love by which to understand divine love.

OUR AGE coined "the-beautiful-people," to describe a very brittle society, and little valued "the unbeautiful." Unless our society learns less shallow values, can see other dimensions of beauty, it will die.

THE MAN with the microscope, the astronomer using a huge telescope, do not see what we casual observers do. But their reality exists beyond our vision. Why should we doubt the Christian vision of humanity merely because it sees beyond the materialistic view?

—TERRY MARTIN

December 25

The angel said to them, "Be not afraid; for behold, I bring you good news of great joy which will come to all the people; for to you is born this day in the city of David a Savior, who is Christ the Lord.

—Luke 2:10-11

"**O**UR Savior is born today, dearly beloved, let us rejoice! For it is not right that we should be sad when it is the birthday of Life. For having taken away the fear of death, Christ fills us with joy because of the eternal life He promises. No one is shut out from a share in this happiness. All of us have one common cause for joy. For Our Lord, the destroyer of sin and death, though He finds no one free from guilt, He comes to liberate all of us.

"LET US GIVE THANKS to God the Father through His Son, in the Holy Spirit, Who has had mercy on us because He has loved us so much. Even when we were dead by sin, He has restored us to life in Christ so that we might be in Him new creatures and new images. Therefore, through this new participation in the life of Christ, now let us put off the old man with his works and renounce the world of the lustful flesh.

"RECOGNIZE, O Christian, your dignity!" — St. Leo the Great (Christmas Sermon).

—FATHER VINCENT A. YZERMANS

December 26

As they were stoning Stephen, he prayed, "Lord Jesus, receive my spirit." And he knelt down and cried with a loud voice, "Lord, do not hold this sin against them." And when he had said this, he fell asleep. —Acts 7:59-60

HOW strange that the Church, after the joyful feast of the Nativity, brings us the feast of St. Stephen, the first martyr after our Lord's crucifixion.

BUT WHAT the Church has done is to wisely remind us that though Our Lord has taken flesh, become incarnate that we might be redeemed, there is much to be asked of us.

LATER in His life, Our Lord is to warn that there are those who will persecute, even kill, those who are to follow Him.

SO QUICKLY, even as we give our thanks for the wonder of the Incarnation, we are reminded we may be asked to make great sacrifices for our faith; that we might be asked to be martyrs, too.

—DALE FRANCIS

December 27

This is the disciple who is bearing witness to these things, and who has written these things; and we know that his testimony is true.
—John 21:24

HOLY Scripture gives us no further biographical data on John the Apostle than that he was the son of Zebedee, and the brother of James. Tradition identifies him with the Beloved Disciple among the twelve and the author of the Fourth Gospel. In art he is symbolized by an eagle, because like an eagle St. John in his Gospel and Epistles soared high and looked deep into the mystery of divine love.

SURELY, all this is correct. Jesus loved John so much that he was permitted to ask who the betrayer would be; and when hanging on the Cross, Jesus entrusted His mother to the care of St. John.

IT IS NOT SURPRISING then that love like this should later express itself in strong words like: "God is love, and he who abides in love abides in God, and God in him" (1 John 4, 16). "Blessed are they who have not seen and yet believe" (John 20, 29).
—FATHER MARTIN SCHOENBERG, O.S.C.

December 28

. . . Herod, when he saw that he had been tricked . . . was in a furious rage, and he sent and killed all the male children in Bethlehem and in all that region who were two years old or under. . . . —Matthew 2:16

THESE innocent martyrs, human sacrifices, were victims of the suspicions, fears, hate and passion of Herod. But they were also victims of Christ's love.

IN THE NATURAL light they were debased; in the supernatural ennobled. Living on earth they might have grown up to be plodding laborers or farmers, perhaps employees of Herod himself, even murderers of Christ. Christ's love saved them. Today mingling gloriously with angels around the throne of God, these innocent victims of Herod's petty fears, are honored amidst the joys of Christmas. Through them earth was made safe for the Babe of Bethlehem and heaven received tiny babes as angels.

CHRIST'S LIFE was preserved. They suffered death, but a death turned into an eternal life of glory. Today they exult in that saving love of Christ.
—FATHER JOSEPH A. VAUGHAN, S.J.

December 29

O my Strength, I will sing praises to thee; for thou, O God, art my fortress. —Psalms 59:9

THERE was a complete change in the life of Thomas Becket. Until 1162 he had been a favorite at the court of England: tall, handsome, outgoing, intelligent, the confidant of the king.

IN 1162 he was ordained Archbishop of Canterbury, because King Henry II wished complete control of the Church in England. Thomas disappointed him. Thomas' life became more austere, he became dedicated to his pastorate, and he consistently defended the Church against interference from Henry.

AS A RESULT the Church maintained its independence in England, and Thomas became a martyr, whose memorial may be noted today, at the command of the angry king.

LORD JESUS, let us stand firmly in the way You wish us to go.
—FATHER GARY LAUENSTEIN, C.SS.R.

December 30

For everything there is a season, and a time for every matter under heaven: . . . a time to rend, and a time to sew; a time to keep silence, and a time to speak. —Ecclesiastes 3:1, 7

SOMEONE has said: "The greatest use of time is to use it for something that will outlast it." That should be our motto as we bring this year to a close. As we look back over the past twelve months we should ask ourselves: "Did I waste any time?" A wasted hour can never be brought back.

"IDLENESS is the devil's workshop," is another well-known phrase. Have we been idle, day-dreaming, or have we kept busy avoiding boredom? Do we spend long hours before the television set or have we decided upon one program a night and spend the remainder of the evening doing something worthwhile?

WE DO WELL to make a few, simple resolutions for the coming year, resolutions that will be beneficial to both body and soul. We ought to resolve to repeat those resolutions each morning.
—FATHER JOHN M. MARTIN, M.M.

December 31

Hear, . . . your father's instruction, and reject not your mother's teaching; for they are a fair garland for your head, and pendants for your neck. —Proverbs 1:8-9

FOLLOWING the Mass on the feast of the Holy Family a little boy sauntered to the Crib in a crowded church and vigorously sang, "Happy Birthday" to Jesus.

AFTER ALL, Christmas was Christ's birthday, so why not be happy for Him? That's the magical delight about those small creatures called children. They are proud of being alive, and want the whole world to know it.

THEIR SONGS, their delights, their unexpected sayings, their happiness — all these are reasons why children are such wonderful things. . . . It is a pity that more parents do not *enjoy* their children.

SO MANY SPEND so much of their time correcting and disciplining and screaming at their children that the over-all effect of obedience is lost. Love and discipline certainly are necessary factors, but we beg you parents, try *enjoying* your children a bit more.

FIND YOUR happiness with, and for them; it will be a deep joy, modeled after the Holy Family's love and mutual help for each other in Nazareth.

—FATHER PETER V. ROGERS, O.M.I.

Index

DOLLEN, Father Charles / Jan. 17, 25 / Feb. 14 / Apr. 16 / July 6, 17

DOYLE, Monsignor Charles Hugo / Oct. 6, 26

DUGAN, Jo Curtis / Apr. 9, 27 / Sept. 6, 30

DUNBAR, Michael / Nov. 6, 28

DWYER, Bishop Robert J. / Mar. 7, 24 / Apr. 14

/E/

EGAN, Marion / Jan. 10, 27 / Aug. 10, 21 / Sept. 5

/F/

FIRST ISSUE, My Daily Visitor (Feb. 1957) / Feb. 20

FISHER, John Julius / May 11, 23 / June 15 / July 10, 18

FITZGERALD, Father Maurus, O.F.M. / Sept. 13, 21

FOY, Father Felician A., O.F.M. / Mar. 15 / May 24, 29 / June 7, 23 / Aug. 4, 12, 22, 30

FRANCIS, Dale / Jan. 13 / Aug. 6 / Dec. 3, 26

/G/

GALLAGHER, Father Joseph / Mar. 1, 29

GINN, Father Roman, O.C.S.O. / Feb. 4 / Apr. 15

GIULIETTI, Julio, M.M. / Aug. 13

GORMAN, Bishop Thomas K. / Aug. 7

GRACE, Mark / Nov. 14, 29

GRUTKA, Bishop Andrew G. / Jan. 1, 7, 23 / Oct. 8, 24

GUSTAFSON, Father G. Joseph, S.S. / Mar. 17 / Apr. 13 / May 3 / June 9, 12, 30 / Aug. 8, 26 / Oct. 12

/H/

HALLINAN, Bishop Paul J. / Jan. 6, 15

HAYES, Betty J. / Oct. 14

HOGAN, Father Joseph F., S.J. / Sept. 26

/I/

ILLIES, Father Wilfred / Feb. 13

/K/

KAISER, Father Edwin G., C.PP.S. / Sept. 12, 17, 27

KELLER, Father James, M.M. / Sept. 16, 22

KENNEDY, Monsignor John S. / Apr. 7, 25

KOCHER, Paul H. / July 5, 31

KOWALSKI, Bishop Rembert C., O.F.M. / Oct. 21

KUTZ, Monsignor Ralph G. / Feb. 29 / Mar. 12, 19, 31 / Oct. 7, 27

/L/

LARKIN, Father Francis, SS.CC. / June 2, 20

LAUENSTEIN, Father Gary, C.SS.R. / Nov. 9, 22 / Dec. 9, 29

LAYNE, Marie / Feb. 16 / Apr. 6, 12, 24 / Aug. 14 / Nov. 18, 25

LEE, Robert G. / May 6, 30

LEUVER, Father Robert J., C.M.F. / Sept. 8

LOUIS, Father Conrad, O.S.B. / June 21

LUX, Monsignor Joseph B. / Aug. 1, 24

LYNCH, Father Kevin A., C.S.P. / June 3, 26
/M/
McBRIDE, Father Alfred A., O. Praem. / Oct. 13
McCARTHY, Father John / Oct. 10, 18
McCORRY, Father Vincent P., S.J. / July 11, 27
McDEVITT, Father Edwin R., M.M. / May 10 / Sept. 2, 29
McKENZIE, Father Leon / Oct. 11, 25
McKUNE, Monsignor J. William / May 2, 20, 25
MADDEN, Father Richard, O.C.D. / Feb. 9, 21
MAGUIRE, Father John R. / Sept. 4, 28
MALLON, Father Vincent P., M.M. / June 11, 22
MALSAM, Margaret H. / June 29 / July 4, 21
MANTON, Father Joseph E., C.SS.R. / Mar. 8, 10, 25 / Aug. 2 /
    Sept. 14
MARLING, Bishop Joseph M., C.PP.S. / May 5, 22
MARTIN, Father John M., M.M. / Dec. 13, 30
MARTIN, Terry / Aug. 18 / Oct. 31 / Dec. 8, 16, 24
MARTIN, Father Tom, S.J. / Apr. 1, 19, 29
MEEHAN, Robert / Dec. 19
MILLER, Father Donald F., C.SS.R. / Feb. 17
MOESLEIN, Father Francis R. / Aug. 16, 29
MORIARTY, Father James D. / Apr. 2, 28
MULLOY, Bishop William T. / May 1, 26
MURPHY, Father Eugene P., S.J. / June 6, 28
MURRAY, Father Albert A., C.S.P. / Apr. 10, 17 / May 8, 15, 18 /
    July 3, 19
MYERS, Father Rawley / Feb. 1, 6, 26 / Apr. 5 / May 14, 28 / Nov. 5, 21
/N/
NEIDHART, Father William J., C.S.C. / Nov. 4, 16
NEVINS, Father Albert J., M.M. / Mar. 3, 22
NIMETH, Father Albert J., O.F.M. / Jan. 2, 20
NOLAN, Monsignor John G. / Jan. 14
NOLAN, Father Joseph T. / Jan. 11, 21
NUSBAUM, Mr. James M., S.J. / Mar. 14
/O/
O'BRIEN, Father John A. / Apr. 3, 26 / Sept. 7, 24
O'MALLEY, Monsignor Edward W. / Feb. 27
O'NEILL, Anne / Dec. 5, 23
/P/
PARIS, Father Charles W. / Mar. 9, 28
PERRY, Father Norman, O.F.M. / Feb. 2, 24
PEYTON, Father Patrick, C.S.C. / Oct. 1, 22
PINGER, Bishop Henry A., O.F.M. / June 1, 19
POLZIN, Theresita / Feb. 8 / June 13, 27 / July 23
PURSLEY, Bishop Leo A. / Feb. 3 / June 5, 18 / Dec. 6, 22

PUTZ, Father Louis J., C.S.C. / Sept. 3, 19
/R/
RAMGE, Father Sebastian V., O.C.D. / Aug. 5, 25
RAYMOND, Father M., O.C.S.O. / Nov. 2, 17, 30
RISKI, Father Bruce, O.F.M., Cap. / Dec. 14, 18
ROGERS, Father Peter V., O.M.I. / Dec. 4, 31
ROXBURGH, Father Gilbert, O.P. / June 10
RUSSELL, Dianne / May 21
/S/
SCHAUER, Father Blase, O.P. / Jan. 4, 18, 24, 26 / Mar. 5, 30
SCHOENBERG, Father Martin, O.S.C. / Dec. 27
SELNER, Father John C., S.S. / Feb. 11, 22 / July 2
SHEEN, Bishop Fulton J. / Mar. 2, 13
SHERIDAN, Father Robert E., M.M. / June 4, 17
SHINE, Very Reverend Bernardine, O.S.B. / Apr. 4, 21
SIEMINSKI, Barbara J. / Apr. 11
SIGUR, Monsignor Alexander / Jan. 8, 30
SMITH, Bishop Leo R. / Mar. 20
SMITH, Father Nicholas P. / July 15, 29
STEVENS, Father Clifford / Jan. 12, 28 / Feb. 12 / Mar. 21
STRAVINSKAS, Rev. Mr. Peter M. / May 31 / Oct. 3
SULLIVAN, James M., M.M. / Mar. 16 / June 16 / July 12
SULLIVAN, James Michael / Jan. 16, 29 / July 28 / Sept. 9 /
    Oct. 30 / Nov. 23
/T/
TANSEY, Anne / Jan. 5, 9, 22, 31 / Sept. 18 / Nov. 3, 13, 27 /
    Dec. 17
THORSEN, Father Robert / Mar. 18
TOBIN, Monsignor Thomas J. / Dec. 11, 21
TORMEY, Father John C. / Feb. 15, 19 / July 13 / Aug. 17 /
    Sept. 10 / Nov. 7
TOURNIER, Monsignor Francis / Dec. 2, 20
TRESE, Father Leo J. / July 8, 14, 30
TUCEK, Monsignor James I. / Aug. 31
/V/
VAUGHAN, Father Joseph A., S.J. / Dec. 12, 28
/W/
WEDGE, Florence / Oct. 29
WELP, Monsignor Harry J. / July 9, 22, 26
WICKHAM, Betty / Jan. 3, 19 / Apr. 23, 30
WILKEN, Father Robert L. / July 7, 20 / Nov. 8, 15
/Y/
YZERMANS, Father Vincent A. / Aug. 15, 20 / Dec. 1, 25
/Z/
ZIMMER, Father Nicholas M. / Nov. 1, 24
ZUROWESTE, Bishop Albert R. / Sept. 15, 25